To the French aristocracy, it was only natural that the King should seek a mistress in place of his staid and unreceptive Queen – although as a commoner Jeanne-Antoinette Poisson seemed an unlikely candidate. But the love affair between Louis XV and the future Madame de Pompadour, which was to last for twenty years, helped to shape the entire history and culture of France.

WORLDS APART

Mansell Collection

LOUIS XV CAME TO THE THRONE AT THE AGE OF FIVE, INHERITING ALL THE GLORY OF THE MONARCHY. BUT HIS MARRIAGE AT 15 WAS A DISAPPOINTMENT WHICH LED TO A SERIES OF ROMANCES AND ULTIMATELY TO THE MOST ENDURING LOVE OF ALL

On 1 September 1715, the Duc de Bouillon walked out on to the balcony of the royal apartments at Versailles, wearing a black feather in his hat. 'The king is dead!' he solemnly declared. He retired for a moment, then reappeared, sporting a bright white feather in place of the black, and cried 'Long live the King!' The new master of France, Louis XV, was a child just five years old.

At his birth, on 15 February 1710, the throne of France was occupied by his great grandfather Louis XIV, the magnificent *Roi Soleil*, the Sun King, who had built the great royal palace of Versailles and reigned France for 72 years. But the young Louis was little over one year old when tragedy struck the family. An outbreak of small-pox and measles swept the royal household, carrying off the little boy's grandfather, father, mother and older brother. Saved by the devoted care of his nurse, who insisted he was too small to be bled as was the custom, the small boy was now not only an orphan, but also Dauphin (Heir Apparent) to the Kingdom of France.

An age of splendour

With such a background, it was not surprising that the young Louis developed a reserved, even secretive personality. His tutors did their work well, however, and his shyness passed for regal dignity, enabling him to carry off any state occasion impressively, despite his dislike of crowds and unfamiliar situations. But although he could be relaxed enough in private, those who offended him, or trespassed emotionally, found themselves turned to stone with a glance or warned off by curt, icy remarks.

As King of France, Louis inherited the aura of splendour that his great grandfather, the Sun King, had built up around the monarchy. 'You are the master here,' his uncle the Regent would tell the little boy. And indeed, the young King soon learned that the world was made for him. Easily

bored, he was always inclined to put his own pleasure and convenience first, without counting the cost to others too carefully. But in spite of his weaknesses, Louis was good-natured, brave, pious, tall, handsome and, above all, a king, so the world would do its best to please him.

At 15 he was deemed ready for marriage, although for reasons of state his bride was chosen for him – in this case by a process of elimination that reduced the list of candidates to one: Marie Leczinska, daughter of the ex-King of Poland. She was seven years older than Louis and by no means a beauty, but he immediately fell in love with her, reputedly giving her seven 'proofs of his tenderness' on their wedding night, and at 17 became the father of twin girls. He eventually had ten children by Marie, of whom a single son and six daughters survived childhood.

👑 *It was thanks to the devoted care of his nurse, Madame Mercier above, that Louis owed his life. Here she receives a portrait of the grateful King*

👑 *The boy king in his coronation robes is shown* right *in a painting by Jean Rigaud which hangs at Versailles. Only five and a half years old when he became King, his was a world ordered by high ceremonial from an early age*

👑 *Louis XV fulfilled his first important public engagement* below *on 12 September 1715. Only five and a half years old and in the care of a Regent, the King attended a Parliamentary session*

Jean-Loup Charmet

♛ *For reasons of politics, Louis married the daughter of the exiled King of Poland in 1725. It was a poor match for the King, as she had neither money, connections, nor youth and looks – but she was good-natured and deeply in love with him. She bore him ten children, of whom six daughters and one son – Louis the Dauphin, seen here – survived infancy*

'Always in bed, always pregnant, always giving birth!'

MARIE LECZINSKA, QUEEN OF FRANCE

For seven or eight years Louis was faithful to his Queen, although she grew increasingly stout, staid and unreceptive. Marie was probably worn out – 'Always in bed, always pregnant, always giving birth!' she grumbled. She was also extremely pious, and although Louis himself was a devout Christian, he found that he needed a different kind of conversation to relieve his chronic boredom and restlessness.

A private life

As a result, disillusioned with marriage and disliking the rigid formality of court life, he was only too glad to spend much of his time away from Versailles at the wide selection of royal hunting lodges and mansions, indulging his passion for the chase, and occasionally attending masked balls, incognito, in Paris.

Meanwhile, Marie kept discovering more saint's days on which it would be improper to have physical relations with her husband, and eventually Louis, still in his twenties, ceased to be faithful. As far as most of his courtiers were concerned, this represented a return to normality, for a French king was expected not only to have mistresses, but to adopt an acknowledged or 'reigning' mistress, the *Maitresse en Titre*.

The prestige of the monarchy was such that this position was not only official, but almost respectable. Competition was fierce, and even the most blue-blooded of courtiers was delighted if a sister or cousin succeeded in captivating the heart of the King.

Louis' first serious affairs demonstrated his

THE RAFFISH REGENCY

Because Louis XV had come to the throne as a child, France was initially governed on his behalf by a regent. This was Philippe, Duc d'Orléans, the little King's uncle – a plump, kindly 41-year-old, whose energy and ambition had long since been sapped by an enormous appetite for wine and women.

The eight years of Philippe's regency changed the entire temper of French society, for the new ruler had no use for the solemn splendours of the Sun King's lengthy reign. Following the Regent's example, society became more openly frivolous and pleasure-loving, and more noted for its good taste than strict morals. Interior decoration took on a lighter, brighter and more intimate air, and charming Rococo curves ousted the ponderous classicism of Louis XIV's time.

When Philippe died in December 1723, despite the rules and rigidities that still characterized life at court, the society over which Madame de Pompadour would preside so elegantly had already come into being.

essentially conservative and domestic nature in an extraordinary fashion, for over a period of years he took each of the three de Nesle sisters as his mistress. Inevitably a Parisian wit asked whether he could be accused of being unfaithful, since he had kept his favours in the family!

Setting the seal on this domesticity, Louis made himself more and more at home at Versailles by building a set of comfortable private apartments behind the vast, draughty rooms which he was supposed to inhabit; stairs led from these apartments to those above, that were home to the reigning mistress.

Bitter humiliation

In this fashion life passed smoothly for the young King, but in 1744 Louis suffered a public humiliation that he never forgot. While campaigning with his army he fell ill at Metz and seemed to be dying. In order to make his peace with God, he banished his reigning mistress (the third de Nesle

Marie-Anne de Mailly Nesle, Duchesse de Châteauroux, represented as daybreak in this painting by Jean-Marc Nattier, was an ambitious woman whose goal it was to make her mark on French history. As mistress to Louis XV, she succeeded in her aim.

Nattier: Mme de Châteauroux. Musée de Beaux Arts. Marseilles/Giraudon

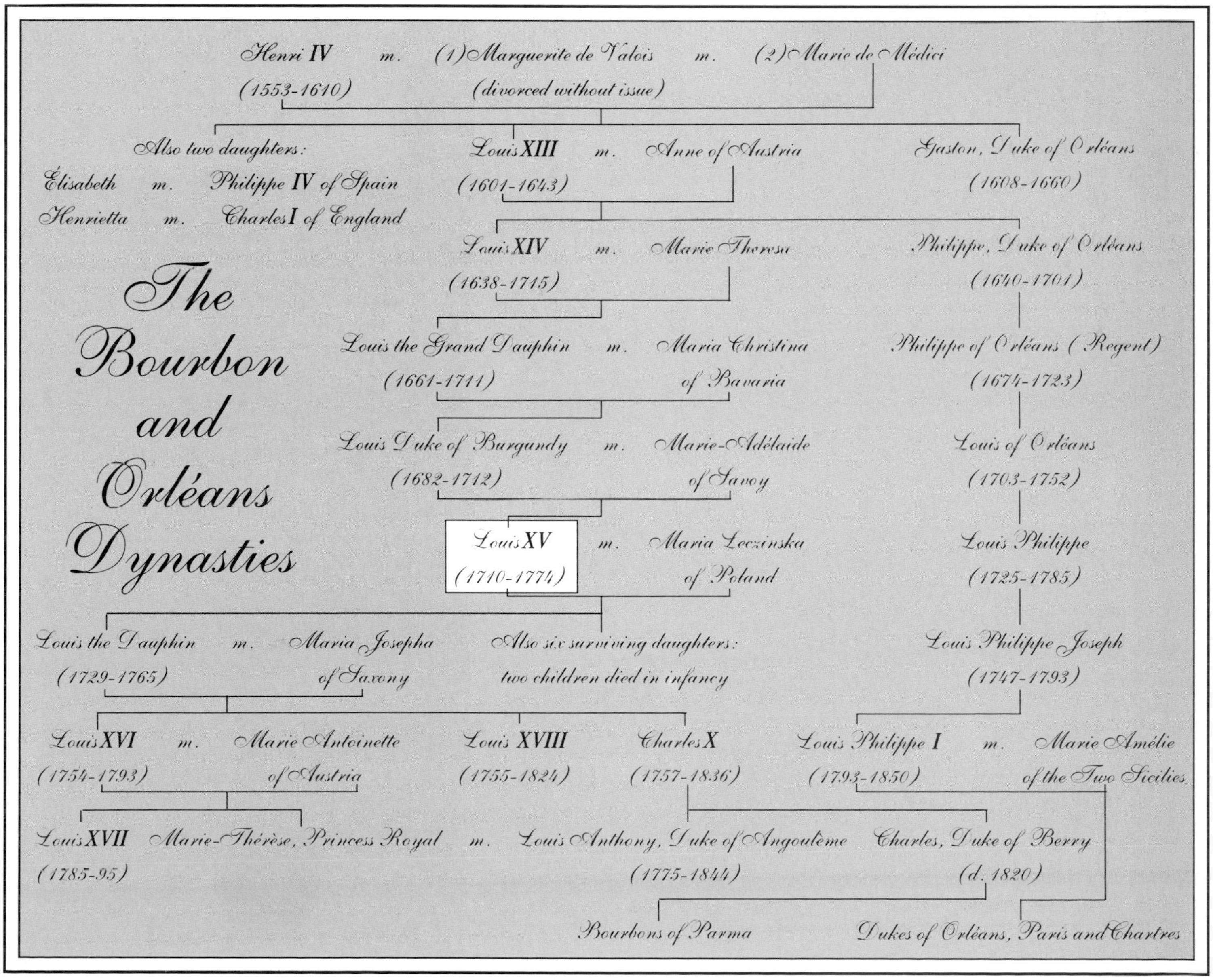

The Bourbon and Orléans Dynasties

Henri IV (1553-1610) m. (1) Marguerite de Valois (divorced without issue) m. (2) Marie de Médici

Also two daughters:
Élisabeth m. Philippe IV of Spain
Henrietta m. Charles I of England

Louis XIII (1601-1643) m. Anne of Austria

Gaston, Duke of Orléans (1608-1660)

Louis XIV (1638-1715) m. Marie Theresa

Philippe, Duke of Orléans (1640-1701)

Louis the Grand Dauphin (1661-1711) m. Maria Christina of Bavaria

Philippe of Orléans (Regent) (1674-1723)

Louis Duke of Burgundy (1682-1712) m. Marie-Adélaïde of Savoy

Louis of Orléans (1703-1752)

Louis XV (1710-1774) m. Maria Leczinska of Poland

Louis Philippe (1725-1785)

Louis the Dauphin (1729-1765) m. Maria Josepha of Saxony

Also six surviving daughters:
two children died in infancy

Louis Philippe Joseph (1747-1793)

Louis XVI (1754-1793) m. Marie Antoinette of Austria

Louis XVIII (1755-1824)

Charles X (1757-1836)

Louis Philippe I (1793-1850) m. Marie Amélie of the Two Sicilies

Louis XVII (1785-95)

Marie-Thérèse, Princess Royal m. Louis Anthony, Duke of Angoulême (1775-1844)

Charles, Duke of Berry (d. 1820)

Bourbons of Parma

Dukes of Orléans, Paris and Chartres

sister, the Duchesse de Châteauroux) and sent for the Queen to receive her forgiveness. He was also persuaded to make a public confession of his sins, which was read in every pulpit in France.

The Well-Beloved

Then, to his embarrassment, he made a complete recovery. The people rejoiced, and it was at this time that the King received his famous nickname, *Louis le Bien-Aimé* – meaning 'Louis the Well-Beloved'. Louis himself angrily banished his officious advisers to the provinces and defied fate by sending for the Duchesse de Châteauroux. Although not well herself, she had a hot bath and rushed out of her house, only to collapse and die soon afterwards of pneumonia.

Unattached once more, Louis was, without knowing it, ready to embark upon the deepest and most enduring of his loves.

♛ *The young Louis, nicknamed 'The Well-Beloved' was a physically active man with a commanding presence, and was seen as a heroic leader of his people. In 1727 François Lemoyne depicted him bringing peace to Europe, in a painting which hangs at Versailles. In fact, his reign was to be marked by a succession of wars, the last of which dragged on for seven years resulting in major French losses*

Lemoyne: Louis XV giving peace to Europe. Versailles/Giraudon/Bridgeman

Louis XV Hunting: Musée de Compiègne/Giraudon/Bridgeman

PLEASURES OF THE CHASE

In the 18th century, hunting was still the pastime of kings, and from his youth onwards Louis XV was an indefatigable rider and an avid follower of the hounds, seen in the tapestry above. The royal forests all around Paris provided abundant quarry – partridges to shoot, boars and wolves to track down, and above all stags to pursue.

Until overtaken by old age, the King is reckoned to have killed an average of 210 stags each year. Always in the best of health, Louis seemed tireless, spending punishing days in the saddle regardless of the weather and terrain. And where the King led, everyone else was obliged to follow. His chief huntsman – an eccentric, privileged gentleman who could get away with remarks for which a duke would have been banished – was heard to complain loudly one day, within the King's hearing, that, 'As usual, he asks if the animals are tired, but he never thinks about the men!'

But for Louis' love of the chase, he might never have met the future Madame de Pompadour, whose husband's château stood in Louis' beloved Sénart forest, giving her the opportunity to follow the hounds and catch the King's eye. Appropriately enough, at the ball where she finally conquered Louis' heart, she appeared dressed as Diana, Goddess of the Chase.

LA REINETTE

Jeanne-Antoinette Poisson was born into the Parisian middle-class on 29 December 1721. Her father, François Poisson, was successful enough as a businessman to set up his family in a fine house on the rue de Richelieu, though he was a gentleman of somewhat questionable character. His prosperity depended on certain services he performed for the influential Pâris brothers – bankers and army suppliers with a finger in every financial pie. It was even rumoured that one of the brothers was Jeanne's true father.

When Jeanne was just four years old, her father was accused of embezzlement and black-market dealings in grain, and was forced to flee into Germany to avoid arrest. Whether he was guilty, or carried the blame for his patrons, is not known. The Poissons' house was seized, but (as François had foreseen) pretty Madame Poisson soon found a protector in a friend of the Pâris brothers, the wealthy Charles François Le Normant de Tournehem.

The perfect lady

François was away for eight years, returning when the charges were finally dropped. He gracefully accepted the presence of de Tournehem as the 'friend of the family,' and in a not untypically 18th-century fashion, the threesome lived together amiably until Madame Poisson's death.

Meanwhile, Jeanne was given the best education that de Tournehem's money could buy.

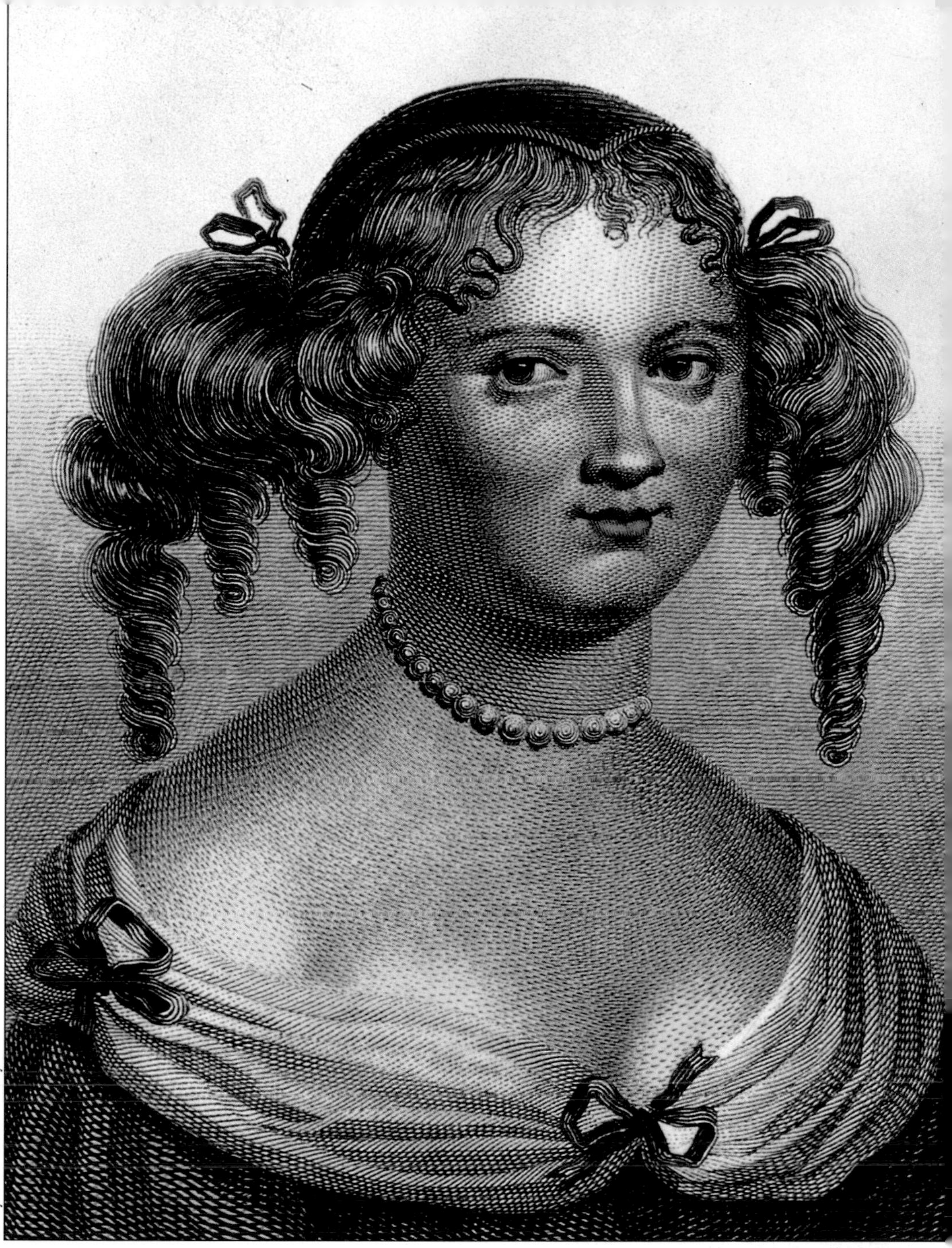

Mary Evans Picture Library

Toque: Le Normant de Tournehem. Versailles/Lauros-Giraudon

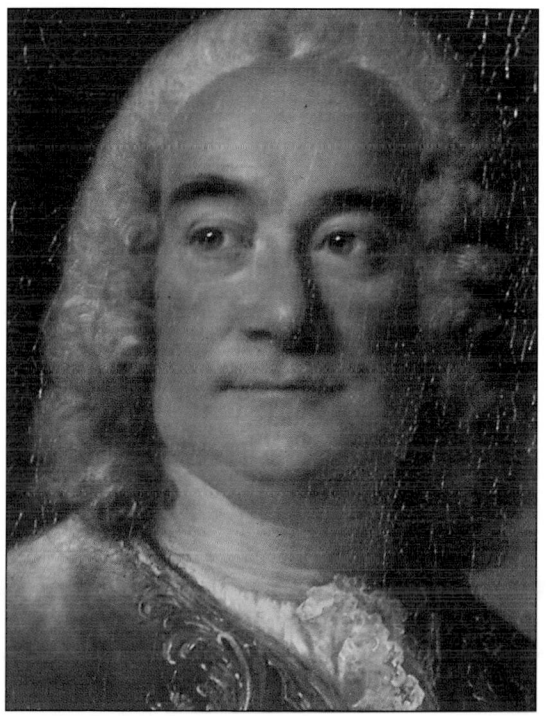

The young Jeanne-Antoinette Poisson came from a prosperous* bourgeois *background (though her father's business affairs were questionable). Remarkably well educated, well spoken and well read, Jeanne was also pretty, charming and a gracious companion. Most significant of all, she also held an early ambition to become the King's mistress.

Charles François Le Normant de Tournehem, depicted by Louis Toqué, rescued the Poisson family in their hour of need. One-time ambassador to Sweden, he was then a Director of the Compagnie des Indes, a* fermier général *or tax collector, and a respected member of the* bourgeois *financial world. He arranged Jeanne's marriage to his nephew Le Normant d'Etioles, a wealthy* bourgeois *with his own estate in the country

Except for a year at a convent, where her health was already giving cause for alarm, she lived at home, studying under tutors of unexpected distinction. She was taught to act and sing by a leading member of the Comédie Française, France's premier theatre company, and learned to speak and recite beautifully from the dramatist Crébillon. She was well read, played the clavichord delightfully, painted, studied botany, collected pets and *objets d'art*, and rode well. Since she was also pretty, charming and a delightful conversationalist, she was – from an 18th-century point of view – as nearly perfect as a woman could hope to be.

These, however, were the qualities that French men valued supremely in love – though not necessarily in marriage, which was much more a matter of status and property. Jeanne's dubious parents were a distinct liability on the marriage market, and the benevolent de Tournehem had to make large financial promises to his nephew, Charles Guillaume Le Normant d'Etioles, before the young man would consent

THE SALON

One of the great French contributions to civilization, the *salon* was an informal gathering where the wise and witty could spend a few hours in agreeable company and good talk. The *salons* first appeared during Louis XIV's reign, but came of age in the 18th century, when elegant conversation was often valued more highly than birth or beauty.

In the most famous *salons*, men of letters and artists rubbed shoulders with politicians, high churchmen and magistrates. The appeal of some houses was enhanced by the hostess's wealth, as with Madame Geoffrin whose thrice-weekly *salons* held out the prospect of a generous gift as well as an excellent dinner. But money was not enough: the truly successful hostess was one who inspired good conversation, guiding but not dominating its course.

One such, Madame du Deffand, was blind. Even more remarkably, Julie de Lespinasse, pock-marked and poor, created a *salon* famed throughout Europe by offering simply her social gifts and a drawing room crammed with sofas, where guests sat and talked from five till nine before going off in search of the supper that Julie could not afford to provide.

Lemonnier: Mme Geoffrin's Salon, Musée de Beaux-Arts, Rouen/Bridgeman

Houdon: Voltaire, Louvre/Giraudon/Bridgeman

♛ *A bust of François Marie Arouet Voltaire, 1694-1778, who became a regular guest at Madame d'Etioles' salons.* It was considered to be a major coup for her to have succeeded in winning over Voltaire, the most famous wit and influential writer of his day

to marry her. But the matter was eventually arranged, and they wed in 1741.

With all her charm it was not long before Jeanne's new husband fell deeply in love with her, and the d'Etioles became a seemingly ideal couple. With no money worries, a town house and a château in the forest of Sénart, they lived an agreeable, leisured life. Jeanne had two children, although only one, a girl named Alexandrine, survived (she died in 1754, at the age of ten).

Success in society

Within three years of her marriage, Jeanne seemed to have achieved every social ambition possible for a woman of her rank. She was received by some of the not entirely blue-blooded members of the aristocracy, and had her own *salon* – a French institution in which the hostess presided over informal gatherings of writers, artists and society people. Conversation was regarded as a fine art and Jeanne d'Etioles brought off a great coup by persuading Voltaire, the wittiest conversationalist in Europe, to become the chief ornament of her *salon*.

She ought to have been happy, and indeed declared that she was. She was deeply attached to Le Normant d'Etioles, and pronounced gaily that she would never leave him – except for the King. No one supposed that she meant it; her

future destiny had been a family joke ever since a fortune-teller had predicted that the nine-year-old Jeanne would become the beloved of a king. As a result, she was given the nickname *Reinette* –'Queenie'. Secretly, she took this seriously, and years later went out of her way to reward the woman who had foreseen her days of glory.

Vain ambition

Madame d'Etioles helped destiny along by doing all that she could to make herself known to the King. Her ambition to become Louis' recognized mistress seemed impossible to achieve, she was a woman of the middle class – a *bourgeoise*. The term – disparaging in the mouth of a courtier – applied equally to the small provincial merchant and the super-rich, highly cultivated giant of finance. Neither, in the final analysis, counted for anything in court society, although an impoverished aristocrat did, on occasion, shamefacedly recoup his fortunes by marrying the daughter of a wealthy *bourgeois*. Unless something quite out of the ordinary occurred, the best that Jeanne d'Etioles could hope for would be a brief liaison in which she might be used and unceremoniously discarded like a woman of the streets.

But fate intervened. Her country house, the Château d'Etioles, stood in the forest of Sénart. So did Choisy, the King's favourite hunting lodge.

Whenever he was there, the d'Etioles were his neighbours, and so entitled to certain small courtesies and attentions. And for the same reason, although such things were never conceded to *bourgeois* persons in any other circumstances, neighbours were permitted to follow the royal hunt in carriages. Jeanne made a point of doing so, turning out in a smart, open four-wheeler which she drove herself with verve and style.

The King had almost certainly heard of the delightful, accomplished Madame d'Etioles, who was such a social success in Paris; at last she had the opportunity to catch his eye.

The rival

Unfortunately Louis was not the only person to notice her, for the Duchesse de Châteauroux realized what she was up to and warned her off in no uncertain terms. Fully aware of the power wielded by a reigning mistress – the position to which she herself aspired – Jeanne obeyed.

The death of the Duchesse in 1744, after Louis' humiliation at Metz, was another stroke of luck. The 'title' was vacant, and although there were many contenders, the King showed no sign of settling down with any of the duchesses whose claims were being discreetly advanced.

No one knows just where or how he came to meet the lovely Madame d'Etioles, but their association was rumoured as early as 1745, during the endless rounds of masked balls with which the court celebrated the marriage of Louis' son. Masked or not, the King was generally easy to spot because of his distinctive gait. But who was the woman with whom he was constantly seen? Was it Madame d'Etioles? And was it serious?

Then, as now, the prospect of a royal romance created a storm of rumour, gossip and speculation among a news-hungry public. Perhaps the climax of the celebrations – the great palace ball planned for February 1745 – would end the rumours and reveal the truth.

Boucher: Mme de Pompadour, Louvre/E.T. Archive

© Collection Viollet

♛ In spite of her unpromising background, the charming and elegant young Madame d'Etioles was soon to catch the eye and capture the heart of the King

♛ Although her birth would not normally have permitted access to royal circles, Madame d'Etioles' château, left, in the forest of Sénart adjoined the King's estate at Choisy – where he had a hunting lodge which he was said to have loved more than any of his palaces. As a country neighbour she was entitled to follow the royal hunting party, a right which gave her the chance to track her own quarry

👑 *Louis XIV,* left, *the Sun King, ruled for 72 years and established the aura of splendour which surrounded the French monarchy. He outlived both his son and grandson, so that his successor, who became Louis XV, was his great grandson*

👑 *Louis XV's father, the* **Duc de Bourgogne** *above, and his wife* **Marie-Adélaide of Savoy** *below both died in the measles epidemic of 1712 when Louis was not yet two years old*

👑 *The* **Grand Dauphin** left, *grandfather of Louis XV also died in the epidemic. He is shown with his wife Maria Christina of Bavaria and their children; the Duc de Bourgogne is standing*

de la Tour: Louis of France, Louvre/Giraudon/Bridgeman

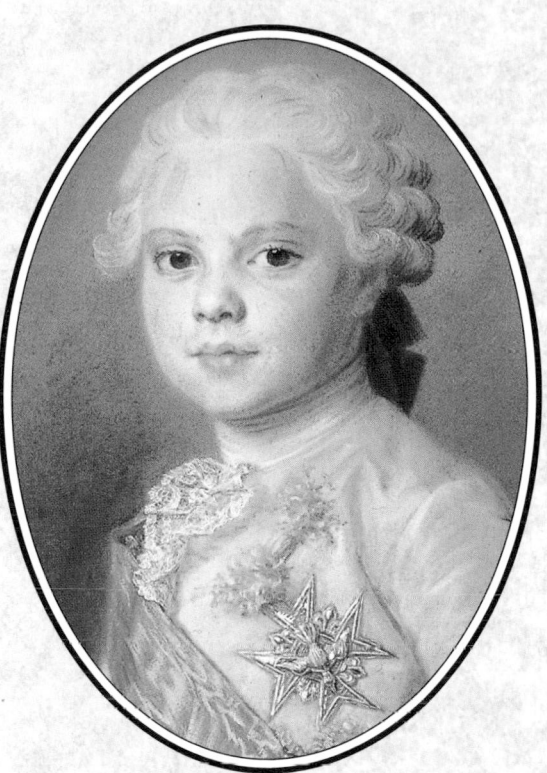

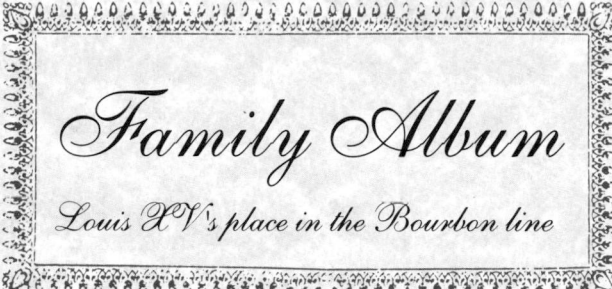

Family Album

Louis XV's place in the Bourbon line

♔ ***Louis XV had only one son, Louis the Dauphin* left. *He died at the age of 36, and did not survive his father, although his son became Louis XVI. The adult Louis the Dauphin is shown* below *in a gold carnet, set with miniatures depicting him together with his wife Maria Josepha of Saxony and his six surviving sisters***

Christie's, London/Bridgeman

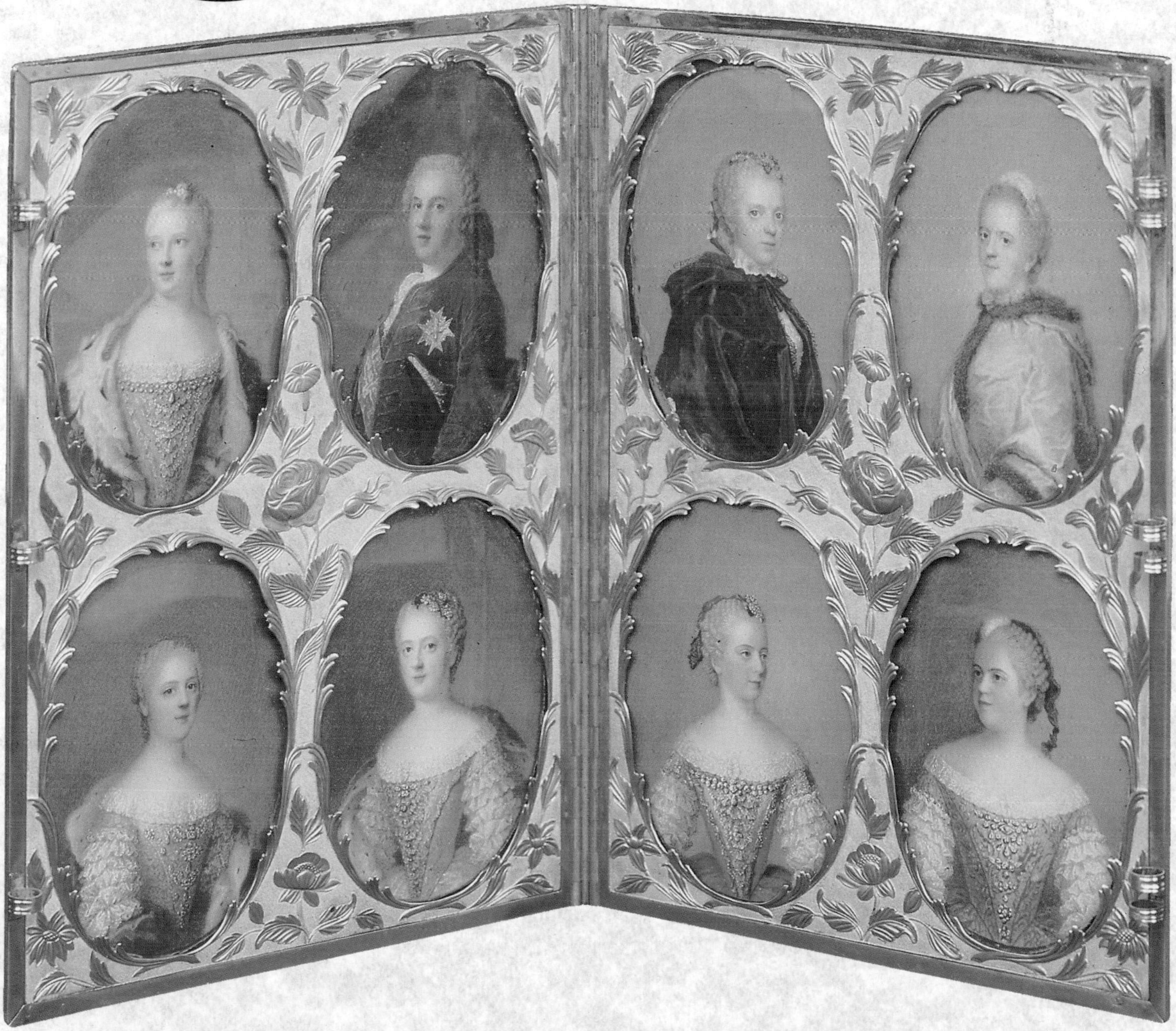

THE AFFAIR BEGINS

**IN A SOCIETY WHERE NOBILITY WAS THE INDISPENSABLE PASSPORT
TO THE COURT, JEANNE POISSON'S AMBITIONS SEEMED DOOMED.
BUT THE YEW TREE BALL OFFERED AN UNEXPECTED OPPORTUNITY
TO JOIN THE PRIVILEGED WORLD OF VERSAILLES**

Vast and glorious, the royal palace dominated the little town of Versailles. It was the symbol of the King's might and majesty, built by Louis XIV at a distance of 10 miles from Paris, beyond the reach or influence of the capital's unruly citizens. The court was an exclusive world, where a thousand highborn nobles scrambled, squabbled and solicited for even the meanest of lodgings within the palace. For them, Versailles was the only place in the universe worth living in, and to be sent back even to the grandest of provincial estates was, in effect, a death sentence, involving execution by humiliation and boredom. Outside Versailles and its inhabitants lay an undifferentiated mass of people who, socially speaking, just didn't exist.

Rich and poor

Curiously enough, along with this social exclusivity went a good deal of physical contact between the upper and lower orders. At Versailles, ordinary people came and went more or less as they pleased. The gates were never shut. In fact, towards the end of the century, when an angry Parisian crowd did get as far as Versailles, the guards found it impossible to close the gates, which had rusted and jammed open through decades of neglect. As a result, traders set up stalls in the yards, vagrants begged near the palatial buildings, and pickpockets frequented the avenues – one got close enough to Louis XV to lift his watch and disappear. In modern terms, security at Versailles was almost non-existent – although perhaps, given the godlike aura of the monarchy, precautions were unnecessary.

Even the most high-toned court entertainments could be almost as open to outsiders. The ball held on 19 February 1745 to celebrate the Dauphin's marriage was perhaps the most spectacular ever held at Versailles, yet no gilt-edged invitations were issued; anyone who could dress up to the occasion was allowed in by the ushers.

The Palace of Versailles in 1722, Versailles/Giraudon/Bridgeman

 **The royal palace of Versailles, above,** the foremost court in Europe and symbol of the King's power and majesty. Versailles was to be the backdrop to a passionate and tempestuous love affair

 **Portrait of the future Marquise de Pompadour, right, by Jean-Marc Nattier.** She is depicted as Diana, Goddess of the Chase, the costume which Madame d'Etioles wore to the Yew Tree Ball

On this occasion, both the entertainment and the speculation about the King's love-life drew a host of party-goers, including many Parisiennes who had learned of Louis' new-found interest in the *bourgeoisie* and hoped to see, or even become the cause of, romantic developments. On the eve of the ball, two endless lines of coaches clattered down the Avenue de Paris into the courtyard.

The masked ball

The crush was so great that the ushers soon gave up attempts to announce new arrivals. The costumed rabble passed through the Queen's rooms, plundered the buffets set out in the surrounding reception rooms, then congregated *en masse* in the ballroom – the dazzling and decadent *Galerie des Glaces*, the Hall of Mirrors. This magnificent chamber's chandeliers were ablaze with thousands of candles that lit up its sumptuous decorations and the throng of masked, extravagantly accoutred guests. Many of them were in fancy dress, decked out as wizards, Chinese ladies and gentlemen, clowns, Turks or shepherdesses. Costumes were elaborate; one 'Chinaman' sported a kind of pagoda on his head, while several 'Turks' had huge composite heads-and-turbans that must have half-stifled them.

'The handkerchief is thrown'

COMMENT ON MADAME d'ETIOLES' APPEARANCE AT THE BALL

Eventually the royal family began to appear. The Queen was resplendent in diamonds and pearls, while her son the Dauphin and his bride, the Dauphine, actually a rather solemn couple, tried to fall in with the mood, dressed as a gardener and a flower-seller. They were unmasked, unlike the royal guests, who included the young Prince Charles Edward – 'Bonnie Prince Charlie', soon to land in Scotland to claim the English throne.

A mask had its uses, for it gave its wearer a welcome anonymity. This allowed eminent people to frolic or misbehave without attracting censure. But this game of disguises cut two ways. During the evening, the Dauphine, a haughty Spaniard, willingly danced with one of her fellow countrymen whose courtly manner and stock of confidential information marked him as an important grandee. Many others, too, fell under the mystery man's spell, but he disappeared without revealing his identity. However, the secret came out the following day – the 'grandee' was in reality a mere cook in a duke's household! The courtiers were hugely delighted at this joke at the Dauphine's expense.

Jean-Loup Charmet

👑 *It was at the Yew Tree Ball, held on 17th February 1745 to mark the Dauphin's first marriage to Marie-Thérèse, Infanta of Spain, that Jeanne Poisson made her first public appearance in the company of the King. The ball, held in the resplendent Hall of Mirrors at Versailles, took its name from the extraordinary costumes adopted by the King and his retinue, who appear on the far left disguised as clipped bushes. Such masked balls were a popular entertainment, which offered the French nobility and their guests such anonymity as they wished to adopt*

PRECEDENCE AND PROTOCOL

Life at Versailles was controlled by a vast list of unwritten laws and facts, impossible to ignore without ridicule or disgrace. Precedence was all-important and sometimes hotly disputed; even Princes of the Blood and foreign ambassadors vied with one another for parking spaces outside the palace, on occasion coming to blows.

With protocol so closely defined, claims were advanced through trivia – the possession of an armchair instead of a chair, a fixed stool instead of a folding one – but every action was watched by suspicious eyes, so that encroachments were generally reported to the King and rapidly countermanded. The court had its own slang and code of behaviour, which imposed cheerfulness on everybody but the royal family; even those banished in disgrace left with a smile and a joke.

It was vital to know who must receive a bow or a curtsey, and who could be put in his place with a perfunctory nod. The more privileged the being, the further his or her sedan chair could penetrate the palace before its occupant was required to alight, adding to the traffic hazard already created by the ladies' wide skirts.

The King himself had yet to honour the party with his presence, but the power of the mask took a new twist when the door of the *Oeil de Boeuf*, his antechamber finally opened. Out came the most extraordinary procession: eight identical yew trees clipped, in the manner of the topiary-work then fashionable, into the shape of a pillar with a large urn on top.

Holes for eyes and mouth in the base of the 'urn' only served to accentuate their bizarre appearance. Evidently, Louis had decided on a form of disguise that, for once, would defy detection; presumably its ludicrous side was overlooked in deference to the royal dignity. Inevitably, this occasion would now go down in history as the Yew Tree Ball.

Once more the disguises had amusing consequences. One ambitious young lady, approached by an amorous tree, rashly assumed that its owner was the King and slipped out into the gardens with him. When she returned, somewhat dishevelled, she was horrified to see Louis, who had removed his headpiece, chatting happily with an unmasked goddess carrying a longbow.

As rumour had suggested, his chosen companion was Madame d'Etioles. It was the equivalent to a public declaration of love – as one courtier put it, 'the handkerchief is thrown'. It was still not clear whether Louis' infatuation would last, or what the status of the new mistress would be. Perhaps she had still not surrendered, for a few days later the King met her at a ball in

👑 *Queen Marie in official court attire. Unlike the King and most of the company she attended her son's wedding unmasked, her dress covered in pearls and with the famous Régent diamond, inset top, sparkling on her hair*

Paris, escorted her back to her lodgings and took his leave. But their public relationship was soon replaced by frequent visits to Versailles during which Madame d'Etioles was said to be petitioning Louis for favours on behalf of her husband.

Ironically, about this time Normant d'Etioles realised what was going on; when his uncle told him Jeanne had become the King's mistress, he fainted clean away. In desperation he wrote begging her to return and she naively showed the letter to Louis. The unsophisticated young Jeanne had not yet understood that he hated to be embarrassed and preferred to keep suffering at a safe distance. He handed the letter back, icily remarking her husband seemed to be a good sort.

Settling in at Versailles

It was a dangerous moment but it quickly passed. By now, Louis was absolutely enchanted by Madame d'Etioles, and increasingly conscious of the fact that she was an ideal companion as well as a lover. Besides, since the death of the Duchesse de Châteauroux he had drifted from one woman to another and he was tired of it.

He brought Jeanne to live in a small apartment at Versailles with a discreet staircase leading to his private quarters, and she began to be seen at informal supper parties to which the

🕊 *The life of the 18th-century French court revolved around romance, intrigue and casual amours, as was popularly depicted in this picture called* Le moment heureux, *the happy moment*

THE HALL OF MIRRORS

'This sort of royal beauty is unique in the world,' wrote Madame de Sevigné of the *Galerie des Glaces*, or Hall of Mirrors, at Versailles. Designed by the architect Jules Mansart, it was the ultimate expression of The Sun King's glory – an enormous gallery, 243 feet long and almost 40 feet high, which became the setting for the grandest events staged at court. Foreign ambassadors trod its daunting length to meet the King, who received them seated upon a dais at one end – but there were also light-hearted occasions like the Yew Tree Ball at which Louis and Madame d'Etioles first appeared together in public.

The Hall takes its name from the 17 tall mirrors along one side, reflecting the view from the arched windows opposite. Although still richly decorated with sprawling, grandiose ceiling frescoes, gilding, trophies of arms and figures holding rock crystal candelabra, the Hall of Mirrors is now relatively bare without the brocades, carpets, furniture, flowers and courtiers that once brought it to life. The French Revolution effectively ended Versailles' history as a residence, but the Hall of Mirrors was occasionally opened – to give a ball for Queen Victoria; as the setting for the proclamation of the German Empire in 1871 by the victorious Prussians; and, in an historic tit-for-tat, as the signing of the peace treaty by a beaten Germany in 1919.

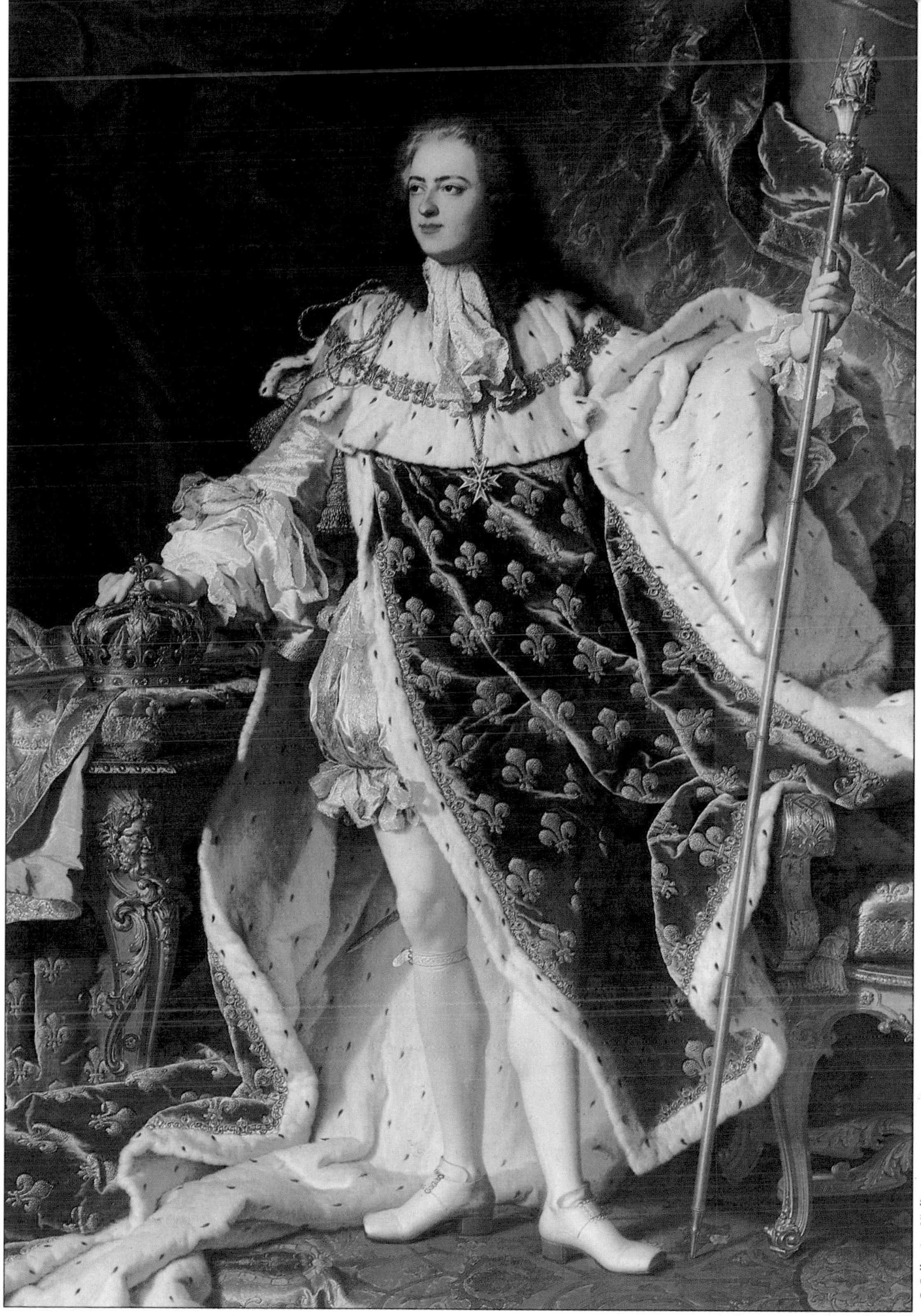

Rigaud: Louis XV, Versailles/Giraudon/Bridgeman

♔ *Louis, seen here in his official regalia, was a majestic figure of a King who commanded the respect of the court and people alike. This portrait by Henri Rigaud (1659-1743) which hangs in the palace of Versailles provides a vivid representation of the splendour of the French monarchy. Little of the King's regalia survives today as it was dispersed following the French Revolution*

© Collection Violet

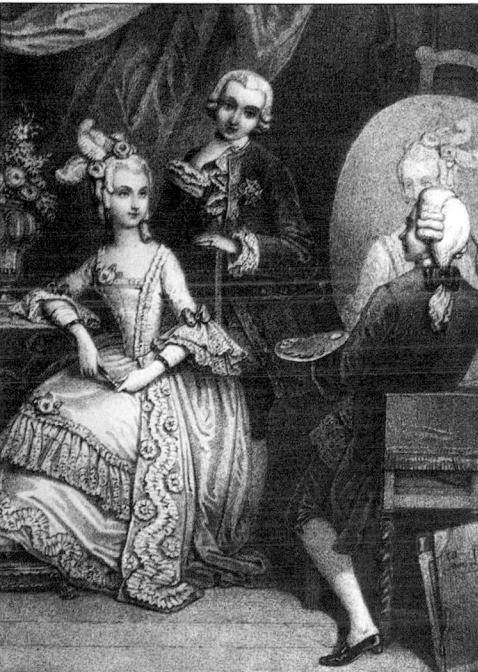

♔ *Madame de Pompadour was a popular subject of the official court painters. In this engraving by Louis Lassalle, she is shown sitting for a portrait by Carle van Loo*

King invited a few close men friends. No doubt this was in the nature of a private test: could the Parisian *bourgeoise*, the child of the rather disreputable Poissons, mix on familiar terms with dukes and counts who had spent their lives at court? Thanks to her careful education she passed the test, in the process making a friend of one of Louis' great cronies, the Duc d'Ayen. That she had not been brought up at Versailles had only one effect of any consequence – it had given her a directness and lightness of spirit that showed to advantage at a court where self-importance and intrigue were so often the rule.

On 3 April 1745, Jeanne made her first public appearance at court. The palace of Versailles had its own theatre, and she was seen in the audience at a performance by the Comédie Italienne. Her presence, resplendent in a box of her own, gave clear notice that her star was still rising. After this, Normant d'Etioles consented to a judicial separation – but he never saw his wife again, and in time found consolation elsewhere.

By the standards of the age, Jeanne could hardly be said to have gone astray, for all her family and friends, including her d'Etioles relatives, were enthusiastic about her new role and happily anticipated the favours she would be able to bestow on them. Moreover, there was no doubt that she was deeply in love with Louis – although the same relatives would presumably have added that any young woman who had the opportunity should fall in love with the King of France!

A PLACE AT COURT

So Jeanne was at last established in the palace but, strictly speaking, not yet at court. Until she had been presented to the royal family, she could have no official place there and no part in its daily round. To accomplish this was not easy, for Versailles was a self-enclosed world with its own customs, hierarchies, intrigues. Courtiers habitually spoke of it as *ce pays-ci*, 'this country', as if Versailles were a separate kingdom. Ignorance of its laws invited the worst of all punishments – ridicule and contempt. Louis was well aware of this and had his own solution. 'It will amuse me to undertake her education,' he declared, with the unconscious arrogance of a born ruler.

Jeanne's royal lover may have made a start on her education, but he was soon called away to campaign with his army in Flanders and left others to carry on with the task. It was only a year since the embarassing proceedings at Metz, so the King and the Dauphin left for battle without female company. Instead, Louis arranged for Jeanne to retire to her own Château d'Etioles at Sénart and spend the summer with her family, preparing for her role as reigning mistress.

To help her studies, the King supplied two tutors, the high-born Marquis de Gontaut and a churchman, the Abbé de Bernis. Although de Bernis had taken holy orders, like so many 18th-century clerics, he was mainly preoccupied with

> ## 'It will amuse me to undertake her education'
>
> ### LOUIS XV ON MADAME d'ETIOLES

worldly advancement. Amiable and obliging, he served Madame d'Etioles well, and she raised him to undreamed-of heights. It says much for her charm and kindliness that, outside the intrigues of the court, both men became – and remained – her devoted well-wishers. No doubt, too, she realized that as a newcomer to the most exclusive club in Europe she might one day have need of friends she could rely on.

The King wrote to her regularly, and one day a letter arrived that was addressed not to Madame d'Etioles, but instead to 'Madame la Marquise de Pompadour'. That letter contained her final passport to the court – the title and estate that she would need to support her position there. Her coat of arms was to be three castles on an

♛ *Madame de la Motte Poisson,* left, *mother of the future Madame de Pompadour, was installed with her in her private apartments; she was overjoyed with her daughter's prestigious new position. Madame Poisson eventually fell victim to cancer and had to face a slow and agonizing death*

© Harlingue-Viollet

♛ *When the King was called away to his military duties in Flanders, the Abbé de Bernis,* below, *was brought in to help the young Madame d'Etioles in her studies. The Abbé remained a close friend of Madame de Pompadour and she, in return, rewarded him with undreamt-of worldly advancement*

FRANC · IOACH · CARD · DE BERNIS

Mansell Collection

azure ground. The Poissons rejoiced in the good fortune of their daughter, and her friend Voltaire wrote a poem to celebrate the occasion.

Louis returned from Flanders in excellent spirits to a rapturous welcome, having been present at the most notable victory of his reign – Fontenoy, where French grit had broken the English army. The King himself had displayed considerable *sang-froid*, at one point suggesting with cool humour to the Dauphin that he should throw back a cannon-ball that had landed nearby.

During the victory celebrations in Paris, dukes scurried to and fro to the palace with tender messages from the King. When the great fête was over, the court returned to Versailles, and Madame de Pompadour followed it at a discreet distance, slipping into her new apartments by a side door. A relaxed Louis supped with her that night. For the moment, his wars were done; her final battle was about to take place.

Vernet: The Battle of Fontenoy. Versailles/Giraudon/Bridgeman

THE ART OF WAR

Though never without its horrors, 18th-century warfare was almost harmless by later standards. It was strictly controlled by rules and conventions, conducted without fanaticism, and restricted to fixed seasons. Relatively small armies manoeuvred carefully in textbook fashion, and it was sometimes claimed that the ideal battle was one in which the outmanoeuvred general appreciated the hopelessness of the position and surrendered before a shot was fired!

In most places ordinary life went on much as usual during a war and balls continued to be held in capitals and courts, regardless of victory or defeat. In these circumstances, Louis XV did not hesitate to campaign with a mistress in tow, or to conduct an absorbing love affair down to the moment at which he left for the front.

True to the cosmopolitan spirit of the age, the finest French general was a German, Marshal Maurice de Saxe. A famous, if doubleedged, example of 18th-century attitudes is the story told of the battle of Fontenoy, at which an English officer is said to have courteously invited the French to fire first; when his French counterpart insisted with equal politeness on giving the English priority, they duly opened up and blew the French line to pieces. Thanks to de Saxe, however, the French recovered and won a great victory at Fontenoy.

Madame de Pompadour set a trend for wearing the bodice cut low and square; this charming day dress, elaborately trimmed with fine lace, is of a style seen in many of her favourite portraits. The wide skirts, typical of court fashion, are supported by two whalebone or cane baskets slung at either hip. These were known as *paniers*, and extended the hips while making the front and back appear flat – considered to give the most flattering silhouette

Hair in Pompadour style, rolled back from forehead, decorated behind with plaits and ribbons

Bodice gives slim, long-waisted look. Open front panel filled with decorative stomacher

Tiny waist achieved with aid of whalebone or cane stays

Elbow-length sleeves with frilly cuffs of chemise protruding

THE AGE OF ELEGANCE

Despite its political setbacks, the 18th-century French court set the taste of the Western world. By the reign of Louis XV the gap had narrowed between the fashion of the nobility and that of the bourgeoisie, and no one was more conscious of this than the lady who had herself moved from the middle-class to royal circles. Thus it was she who gave the name 'Pompadour' to a whole new style

This beautiful *robe de ville* shows an 18th-century gown at its most modest and informal; the hoops of the skirt have risen up as the wearer sits down. It is made of silk – a very popular, but costly fabric on which the rich would spend an enormous amount

V- shaped opening in front of skirt displays large area of petticoat- often more elaborate than dress itself. Even plain dresses show an underskirt

(colour retouching by Bill Payne)

after Boucher: Anne de Pompadour/Victoria and Albert Museum

THE PASSIONATE YEARS

**SECURE IN THE KING'S FAVOUR, MADAME DE POMPADOUR
ESTABLISHED HERSELF AT VERSAILLES IN THE TEETH OF MANY
JEALOUSIES AND INTRIGUES. WITH HER AS HIS COMPANION, LOUIS
FOUND A NEW DELIGHT IN DOMESTICITY AND THE ARTS.**

Ollivier: Chez le Prince de Conti, Louvre/Lauros-Giraudon

T he state apartments were crowded with onlookers on the day that Madame de Pompadour was presented at court. They had come to see an unusual and perhaps sensational show. As the first *bourgeoise* royal mistress, the new Marquise could expect her every movement to be scrutinized and her every mistake noted and set down against her; the courtiers had their own ideas as to what constituted amusement, and even those who had nothing against her were probably hoping that there would be some agreeable disaster – a word out of place, a clumsy gesture, a trip with unlucky consequences.

On the whole they were disappointed. Everything went off decorously enough, although the sense of strain could hardly be missed. Going from room to room with the swift gliding walk characteristic of the court lady, the Marquise was introduced in turn to the King, the Queen and the Dauphin; her sponsor was the irreproachably blue-blooded Princesse de Conti, whose objections to the office had been overcome by a promise from the King to pay off her mountainous gambling debts.

Audience with the Queen

During the proceedings, only the King seemed to be embarrassed, dismissing the Marquise after a few muttered words; a stranger might have believed that he disapproved of the entire business. By contrast, the Queen declined to give the courtiers anything to snigger about. She greeted the newcomer kindly, and tactfully enquired for news concerning a mutual acquaintance. Madame de Pompadour replied with grateful

👑 *The courtier chosen to present the newly ennobled Marquise de Pompadour to the Queen was the Princesse de Conti, seen above left in her apartment.*

👑 *Madame de Pompadour, right, in a portrait by court-painter François Boucher, was taken aback by the unexpectedly kind reception of the Queen Marie Leczinska, above; she responded with assurances of her love and her wish to please. For her part, the Queen confessed herself relieved that her husband's new mistress was at the very least respectful – unlike the last one, who had treated her with a mixture of insolence and neglect*

ardour, and incredulous courtiers noted that as many as twelve sentences had been exchanged by the time the interview came to an end, Queen Marie reflecting perhaps that the *bourgeoise* Marquise could hardly be worse than the well-born Duchesse de Châteauroux, who had treated her with a wounding mixture of insolence and neglect. In fact, the Queen did later reap the benefits of Madame de Pompadour's kindness.

The Marquise's final audience, with the King's son, was something of an anti-climax. The Dauphin, who disapproved of his father's immoral habits, addressed a single sentence to her before indicating that the interview was over; it was said afterwards that he stuck his tongue out at her as she left, but this seems unlikely. What mattered was that she had come through the presentation with only a single trivial mishap (a dropped bracelet), and was now a full member of the court.

Almost at once, Louis carried her off for a 'honeymoon' in the intimacy of Choisy, with only a handful of friends for company. All went well until the King became ill, mainly through

> ## 'If there must be a mistress, better her than anyone else'
>
> QUEEN MARIE

Nattier: Louis XV, Hermitage Museum, Leningrad/Robert Harding

🔹 *Casanova met the King, above, around 1750. He recalled that Louis had the most magnificent head and expression he had ever seen – and said that not even the most skillful painter had done it justice. As he saw Louis, he remarked on his combination of beauty and grace, and did not doubt for a moment that Madame de Pompadour had truly been in love with him*

🔹 *The King's lever (French for rising), left, when he rose from his bed in the morning was one of the principal ceremonial events of the day, attended by a retinue of valets and nobles. At night, when it was time for the King's coucher, the rigmarole was reversed with the same degree of public attention*

Mansell Collection

A PRIVATE WORLD

To escape from the court, Louis XV fitted out a private suite within the palace of Versailles. For a long time he delighted in the *Petits Appartements* – the little rooms, constructed high up on the second floor; jealous courtiers who could not gain admittance called these chambers 'the rat's nest'.

This mansion in miniature had every convenience, including a library, a bakery where Louis made his own pastries, and a workroom in which he turned ivory on a lathe and made watches. From the *Petits Appartements*, the King could take the stairs up to a dining room and walk round the courtyard at rooftop level. A different set of stairs led him up to attic suite of Madame de Pompadour, exquisitely furnished and crammed with interesting things. The Marquise herself reached the suite in a chair lift which her servants hauled up a shaft.

Among the most interesting features of her apartments was a little room above them, occupied by her maid, Madame de Hausset, who habitually listened to the Marquise's conversations with the King and others, noting down what she heard. Almost consigned to the flames after Madame de Pompadour's death, these memoirs remain the most intimate account we possess of a gifted woman and a memorable relationship.

Mansell Collection

---

self-indulgence, and the Queen dutifully came to came to see him. However resigned she may have been to Madame de Pompadour's role, she was not entirely happy to be dining at the same table as her husband's mistress, and the atmosphere was strained until she made up her mind to leave. Louis recovered with no ill-effects and the honeymoon ended on a happy note. Then the lovers rejoined the court at Fontainebleau for the ritual six weeks' hunting in October and November, before returning to Versailles.

Ceremonial routine

However often they played truant from it, the palace was now the centre of both their lives. The King in particular was imprisoned in a straightjacket of ceremonial duties, beginning each day with his *lever*, at which he got out of bed, washed and dressed with the assistance of a group of valets and nobles, each determined to maintain his rights in such a matter as helping him into his silk shirts and handing him his wig. On his way to the Chapel, in council or seated at dinner, the same unvarying protocol had to be observed. At night, when it was time for the King's *coucher*, the morning's procedure was

reversed and he was undressed and put to bed with the same public attention.

Louis disliked all the fuss, and found the state apartments oppressively vast and uncomfortably chilly. Characteristically, he was unwilling to interfere with established court routines, but instead contrived to create a second, private life that he could live behind the official façade of his public activities.

'To separate Louis de Bourbon from the King of France', wrote a contemporary, 'was what His Majesty found most irksome in his royal existence.' Every night, after dutifully allowing himself to be bedded at the *coucher*, Louis got up again and went to sup or sleep in comfort in the private apartments. His one innovation in the routine of the court was to vary the time of the next day's *lever*, which he fixed earlier or later, depending on his nocturnal schedule; and whatever else happened, before the first valet appeared in the royal bedroom, Louis had always slipped back between the official sheets and was ready to be ceremoniously woken and dressed.

Everybody knew what was happening, but the ancestral bed had been honoured, the privileged shirt-holders and candle-bearers satisfied,

> ## 'To separate Louis from the King of France was what His Majesty found most irksome'
>
> COURT MEMOIRS

Jean-Loup Charmet

Roslin: The Duc de Richelieu, Staatliche Museen, Berlin/Robert Harding

♛ *Madame de Pompadour's early training had given her an unmatched talent for acting and singing. Here she performs* Acis et Galatée *in her private theatre in the Petits Appartements at Versailles. The original theatre at court had accommodated only fourteen spectators, but Madame de Pompadour's delight in acting led her to petition the King until he consented to have a much larger auditorium built*

♛ *One of the few who were not captivated by Madame de Pompadour was the Duc de Richelieu. A firm friend of the King's and a regular fixture of court life, he was handsome, charming, wicked and corrupt. Few things were ever denied him; the Regent's mother remarked, 'If I believed in sorcery I should think that the Duke must possess some supernatural secret, for I have never known a woman to oppose the least resistance to him'*

and public appearances had been kept up – which to the 18th-century French court was the most important consideration of all.

Private lives

By contrast with the gilded grandeur of the state rooms, Louis' private apartments were light-hearted and unpretentious, with lower ceilings, plainer walls and an emphasis on pastel shades and delicate carving; they were, in fact, decorated in the style that came to be known as *Louis Quinze*, after their royal patron.

From here it was only a short trip up a staircase to the suite of rooms occupied by Madame de Pompadour. They had previously been occupied by the Duchesse de Châteauroux, whose untimely death had made possible Jeanne d'Etioles' meteoric rise; but memories of the earlier mistress were soon banished as Madame de Pompadour put the imprint of her personality on her new quarters, filling them with the flowers, pets, nick-nacks and *objets d'art* which she accumulated with a true collector's passion. Like the King, she had courtesy calls and other duties to perform, but for most of the time she managed to be at home in her apartments, reading, writing, receiving calls – and ready to devote herself exclusively to Louis if he chose to visit her. He came often, without warning, and whenever he did so the Marquise's visitors instantly departed, leaving the lovers alone together.

Making friends

During the first five years of their long relationship, they were visibly in love and happy. Moreover they were in the prime of life – the King, handsome and fascinatingly husky voiced, still in his thirties, the Marquise not yet worn down by ill health, deliciously pretty, with a vivacity and charm which, we are assured, none of her many portraits managed to capture.

Despite the Marquise's title, her origins were not forgotten, and snobbish courtiers enjoyed making play with her surname (in French, Poisson means 'fish'), but she was shrewd enough to flaunt rather than conceal it, letting the world see how much she liked china and other ornaments with pronounced aquatic decoration! She had her own team of supporters in her companion and friend Madame d'Estrades (a cousin of Le Normant d'Etioles), her maid, her

C. van Loo: La Conversation Espagnole, Musée des Arts Decoratifs, Paris/Robert Harding

'You are the most delicious woman in France'

LOUIS XV TO MADAME DE POMPADOUR

doctor and a cousin in the service of the Dauphin, the Sieur Binet, who seems to have been helpful during the early stages of her relationship with the King. Most of Louis' close friends quickly took to the Marquise and thoroughly enjoyed the intimate dinner parties held in the King's apartments.

Making enemies

Among those who remained Madame de Pompadour's enemies were two talented talkers and wits, the reprobate Duc de Richelieu – always in and out of the Bastille and ladies' bedchambers – and the Minister for the Navy, the Comte de Maurepas. The Marquise, cleverer and more amusing than previous royal mistresses,

seems to have offended them by unintentionally stealing some of their limelight. The Dauphin too remained hostile, but the Queen appreciated the newcomer's desire to please, remarking that, 'If there must be a mistress, better her than anyone else,' and in time it was the mistress who persuaded the King to show his neglected spouse more kindness and consideration.

The Marquise attempted with less success to conciliate Richelieu, and was forced to tolerate his barbed remarks, knowing that the King would forgive him anything. But she did not always turn the other cheek. When she found that de Maurepas was circulating rude verses about her, a sharp battle ensued, and it was the minister who woke one morning to receive a brief formal message from the King directing him to retire to his estate. Evidently anxious lest some hint of his old friend Maurepas' existence should cast a shadow over his own pleasures, Louis wrote, 'Since your estate at Pontchartrain is too near, I request you to retire to Bourges this week without having seen anyone but close relations.'

Such deadly encounters were to recur every few years, usually without causing more than a momentary ripple in the smooth, affable surface

♛ *The painting* above, *called the* **Conversation Espagnole,** *depicts* **Madame de Pompadour,** *left, dressed as a Spanish lady. One of a pair painted by Carle van Loo, it was left by the Marquise to her brother, the Marquis de Marigny, who said that they were the only portraits to give a true likeness of her. It was reported that her beauty was as much a matter of charm and vivacity as of bone structure, making it no simple matter to capture on canvas*

of life at Versailles. Meanwhile the King, so taciturn and withdrawn in public, relaxed and even made merry when the doors had been shut on the court. Few but his most intimate friends saw this side of his personality, although small parties of courtiers were admitted to dine on days when Louis had hunted. But it was not easy to gain access. Hopefuls crowded round the door, waiting for a glimpse of the King, who had been handed a list of 'possibles' by Madame de Pompadour. When he did open the door he merely glanced round, retreated, and checked off some names on the list. An usher summoned the fortunate few while the rest slunk away.

Like so many rituals at Versailles, proceedings seem to have been deliberately designed to promote subservience and envy. This made the

♛ *The 18th-century fashion for the cultural salon led to a rebirth of interest in patronage of the arts. The larger picture on display is the Boucher portrait of Madame de Pompadour shown on page 23*

♛ *Madame de Pompadour was one of François Boucher's great admirers. The painting* right, *called* Venus and Mars surprised by Vulcan, *was once owned by the Marquise herself*

E.T. Archive

THE GAMBLING DEN

Although those who lived at Versailles considered themselves rare and privileged beings, life in the palace offered few pleasures beyond petty intrigue and lovemaking, both of which flourished mightily. One way of filling an empty evening was to set out card tables and play for stakes – a pastime so popular with generation after generation of bored aristocrats that Versailles was nicknamed 'the gambling den'.

Almost everybody gambled, even including Louis XV's pious Queen Marie Leczinska, who characteristically remained faithful to a dice game called cavagnole long after it had gone out of fashion. By this time most people preferred card games – whist, piquet, comet – most of which required a certain degree of skill; being obliged to play with

the Queen embarrassed modish courtiers, although they were presumably happy enough to take her money. Marie lost large enough sums to get seriously into debt and to stay there until Madame de Pompadour persuaded the King to come to her rescue.

Stakes as a rule were high, and not every loser was able to pay up at once; the King himself won such large amounts at piquet that he had to allow the debtors time to pay. Another victim of the gambling bug was the Princesse de Conti, who in return for the King settling her debts, was compelled to demean herself by presenting the upstart Madame de Pompadour at court. Perhaps warned by her example, the Marquise seems never to have cared much for 'great golden play'.

Mansell Collection

happy informality found inside the apartments all the more striking. The only detailed description of a hunting supper was written by the Prince de Croy, who was relieved to find rumours of wild orgies behind closed doors were unfounded. In fact the atmosphere was almost domestic,'with great freedom and no excess.' Only two or three servants waited at table.

The prince wrote, 'the King was relaxed and happy, but always with a certain grandeur which one could not fail to notice; he did not appear in the least shy, but very much at home.' Afterwards Louis went into the next room, where he personally made and poured coffee, evidently enjoying the absence of servants. Three tables were set out and the party played cards until one o'clock, when a sleepy Madame de Pompadour finally persuaded the King that it was time for bed.

'The King was relaxed and happy, but always with a certain grandeur'

THE PRINCE DE CROY

A privileged few were also allowed to watch or take part in the private theatricals which Madame de Pompadour began to put on in 1747. Since the courtiers had been expensively educated to speak, sing and play a musical instrument, the performances were highly professional as well as extremely socially select – four of the five male parts on the opening night of the first production, Molière's *Tartuffe*, were taken by dukes! To begin with, a tiny theatre was built in the King's private apartments; as ever, exclusiveness was the keynote, with room for no more than 14 spectators. But the productions were so successful that the King relented and permitted a more spacious theatre to be constructed in the well of a rarely used staircase.

Amusing the King
In all this, Madame de Pompadour's early training proved invaluable. Given her position, it was inevitable that she should take the leading female role in every production; what could not have been foreseen was that she so obviously merited it, acting and singing with an unmatched charm and skill. After one performance, in a rare display of emotion in the presence of other people, the King kissed her and exclaimed, 'You are the most delicious woman in France!'

But even in these happy years he remained a moody individual. One danger sign was that his skin took on a yellowish tinge – whether from boredom or an out-of-condition liver – and then

Boucher: Venus and Mars surprised by Vulcan/The Wallace Collection

♛ *It was partly because of her own accomplishment in the arts that Madame de Pompadour commanded such respect and wielded such influence among the artistic community. The engraving,* far right, *called* Vénus et l'Amour *was done by the Marquise herself in 1752. The similar ivory carving of a Bacchanalian scene is from the lid of a box which she owned. It is not known whether the engraving was inspired by the box or the other way round; one possible interpretation is that it is an early design study from which the box was commissioned*

Robert Harding Picture Library

© Collection Viollet

♛ *The Marquise devoted great effort to her art. This charming etching was completed under the direction of Boucher, the painter she so much admired*

Roger-Viollet

the Marquise would drive away ministers and petitioners, and set herself out to cure him. Even so, there were occasions when he was so determined to be miserable that he would command her: 'Do not make me laugh today!'

The prohibition was necessary because she was so unfailingly successful at amusing him. They certainly loved each other, but Madame de Pompadour never supposed that loving was her only duty. In fact she worked very hard to keep the King happy – because of her love, because his temperament was so strange and difficult and, no doubt, because her position depended on his continuing affection and approval.

Studied charms

Going to bed late and rising early, riding with him, travelling with him, she was always there when he needed her, although the constant effort to keep up with the exceptionally strong and active King strained her already fragile health. As a companion she had many advantages over his earlier mistresses; far less greedy and domineering, she was also less preoccupied with her own importance, surprising Louis with her sprightly, informal remarks and ready wit.

She may very well have studied her effects, preparing conversational gambits, jokes and stories for Louis' entertainment, just as she prepared the menus for their suppers. Both of them had a taste for news of crime, and snippets of scandal and gossip, dutifully reported by the censor who read every letter that entered or left Versailles.

It was typical of Louis' style of government that he liked to know what was going on, but never did anything about the bribes and rake-offs his courtiers' correspondence revealed. When an unusually energetic minister proposed reform, the King replied, 'Yes, the thieving is enormous. But calm yourself: the evil is incurable.' A wish to alleviate his boredom, not moral zeal, inspired interest in the activities of his subjects.

A woman of the world

Madame de Pompadour was wise enough to realize that all the charm in the world would not bind the King to her unless she could bring new interests into his life and share them with him. Since he found kingship a chore, he had few really satisfying occupations other than hunting with which to fill his life. He was not fond of books, and he fought shy of the intellectuals whose company the Marquise enjoyed. When she suggested inviting an author to supper, Louis wriggled out of it by arguing that France had so many great writers that if one of them dined at the King's table, the rest would form a never-ending queue.

But Louis did have a taste for building and decorating, as his private apartments showed; and Madame de Pompadour did everything in her power to encourage it. She herself was a passionate collector and builder, perpetually acquiring new treasures, putting up and altering houses, decorating and then redecorating. Increasingly the King, too, found that there was no happiness like devising new projects, poring over the plans and collecting the contents for a new house.

Patron of the arts

Since France boasted such great architects as Jacques Ange Gabriel, great painters such as François Boucher, and legions of fine craftsmen working in wood, metal, porcelain, enamels and precious stones, Louis XV and Madame de Pompadour were able to leave behind a heritage of superb buildings and works of art. These were incredibly expensive pastimes, adding to the financial problems which would eventually cost the monarchy dear. Louis XV was sometimes dimly aware of France's various ills, but remarked accurately enough that 'It will last my time.'

For now, whenever he had a spare moment, he hurried up the staircase to the Marquise's rooms, an enchantingly perfumed and flower-filled refuge, which always held the most charming and interesting of women, new and lovely things to look at, and many agreeable choices to make. Here, at least, Louis was never bored. One of the Marquise's friends remarked that, whatever the exact nature of their relationship, Louis would never leave her. The future would reveal just how accurate this prediction was.

Courtly life was never anything but grand and lavish. This supper menu card for Saturday 4 November 1757 includes a range of eight different hors d'oeuvres and a similar choice of roast meats

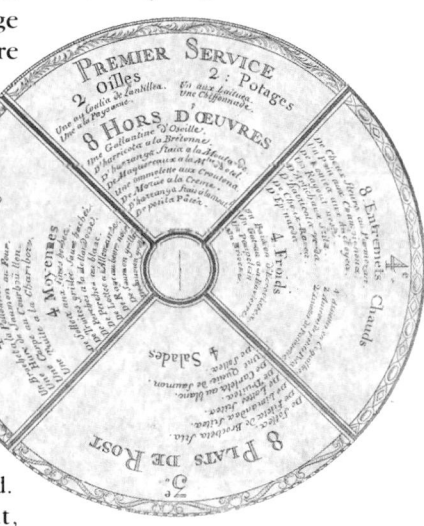

VUE DE LA MAISON ROYALLE DE CHOISY DU CÔTÉ DU JARDIN
Le Roy qui prend, ajoust a cette maison, y fait tous les jours quelque changements, a l'enbeli beaucoup par de nouveaux batimens.

ROYAL CHATEAUX

Versailles was the centre of France's court and government, but there were many other royal residences within easy reach. Lacking the taste for public life, Louis XV was always happy to retreat to these havens from the overpowering formality of the court.

Most of all he enjoyed escaping to smaller houses where he could live informally with Madame de Pompadour and a group of chosen friends. Choisy, in the forest of Sénart was Louis' own creation, and his long-time favourite – but he also regularly visited Marly and La Muette, Trianon, as well as Madame de Pompadour's houses at Crécy and Bellevue. For the King, privacy was a luxury, and at Choisy he even installed machinery that carried food in and out of the room, without the need for (visible) servants.

The informality, like the smallness of the houses, was only relative; guests at each residence wore uniform, and at Choisy the King decreed Madame de Pompadour's writer friends must dine apart from his own circle!

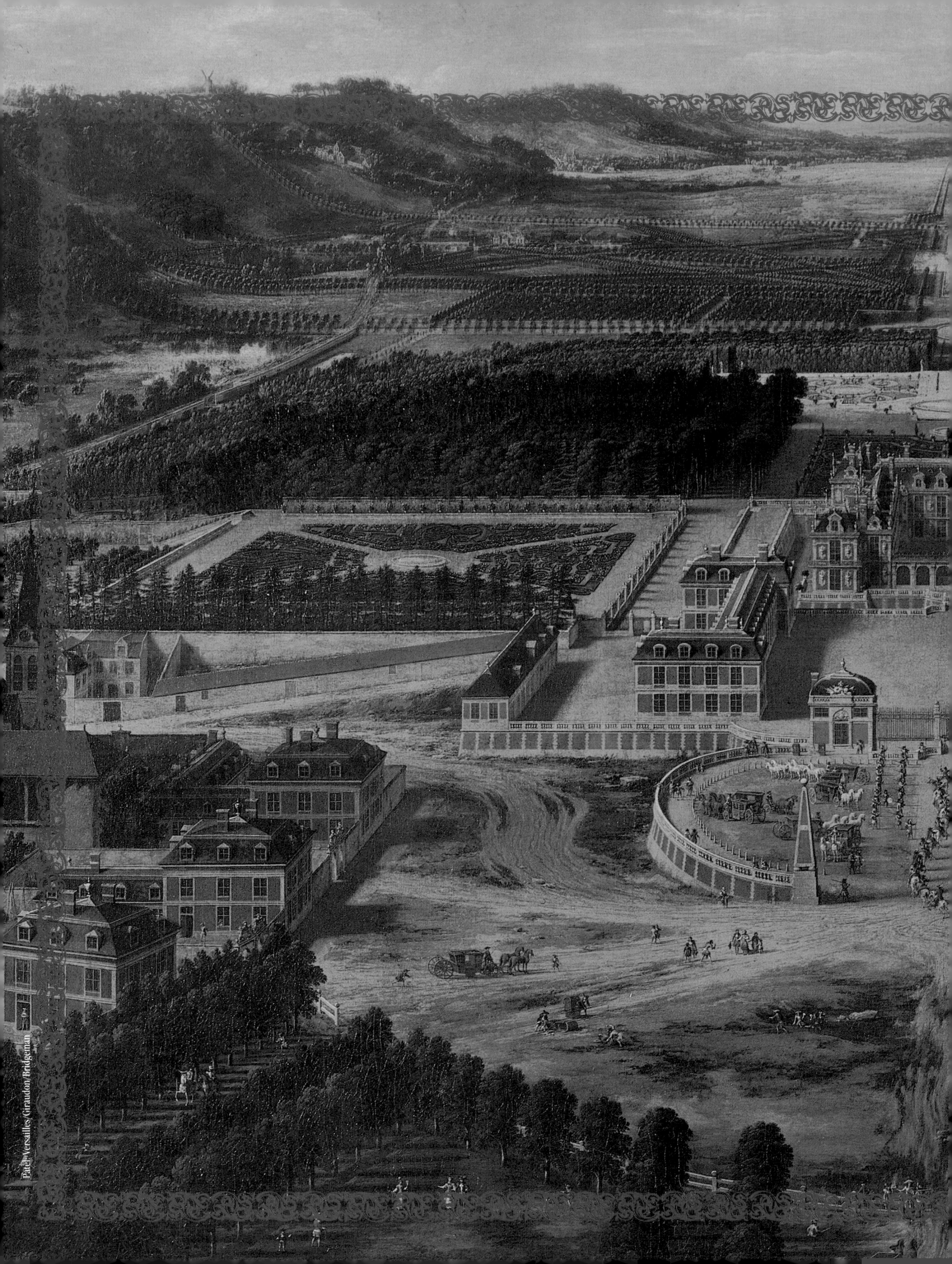

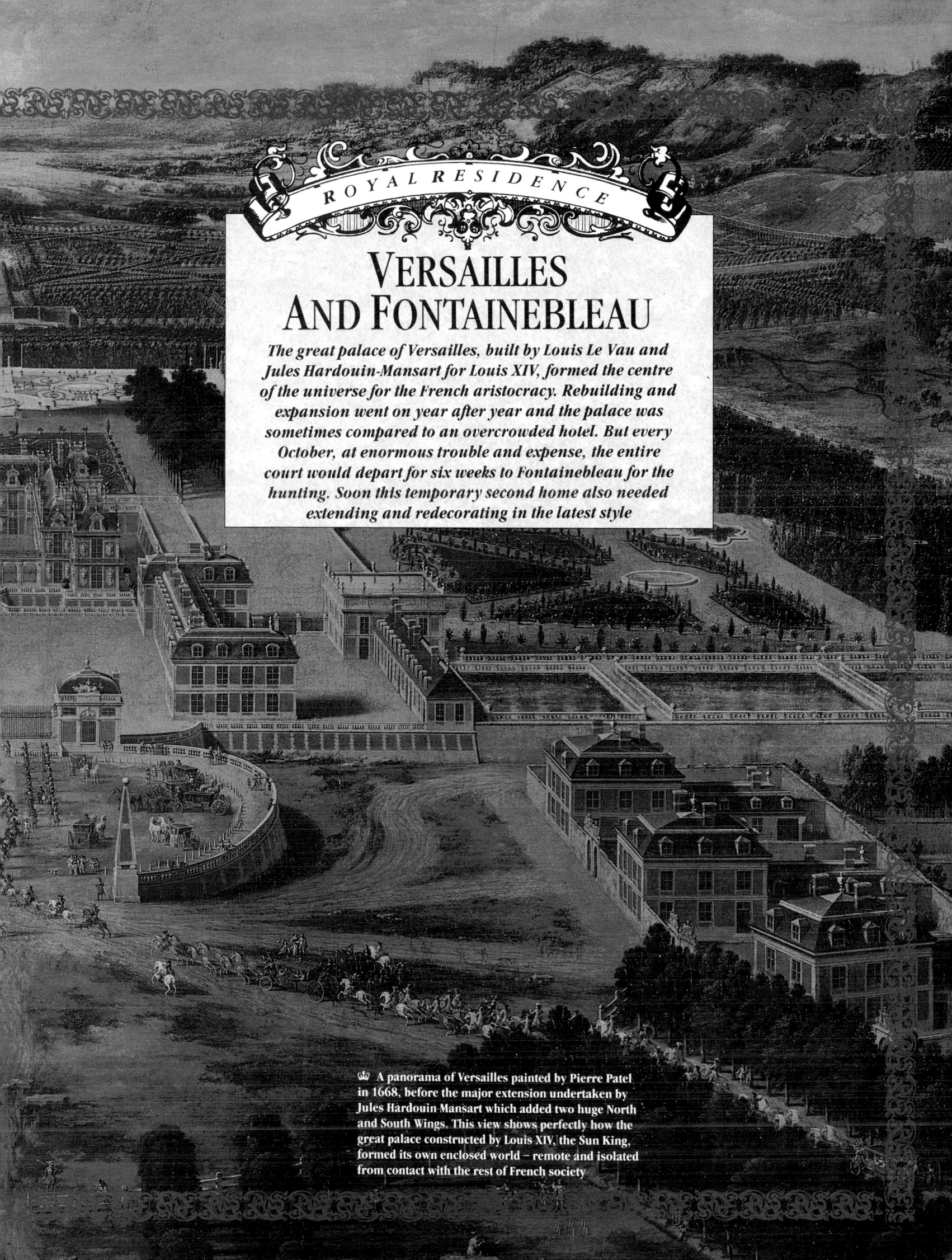

VERSAILLES AND FONTAINEBLEAU

The great palace of Versailles, built by Louis Le Vau and Jules Hardouin-Mansart for Louis XIV, formed the centre of the universe for the French aristocracy. Rebuilding and expansion went on year after year and the palace was sometimes compared to an overcrowded hotel. But every October, at enormous trouble and expense, the entire court would depart for six weeks to Fontainebleau for the hunting. Soon this temporary second home also needed extending and redecorating in the latest style

A panorama of Versailles painted by Pierre Patel in 1668, before the major extension undertaken by Jules Hardouin-Mansart which added two huge North and South Wings. This view shows perfectly how the great palace constructed by Louis XIV, the Sun King, formed its own enclosed world – remote and isolated from contact with the rest of French society

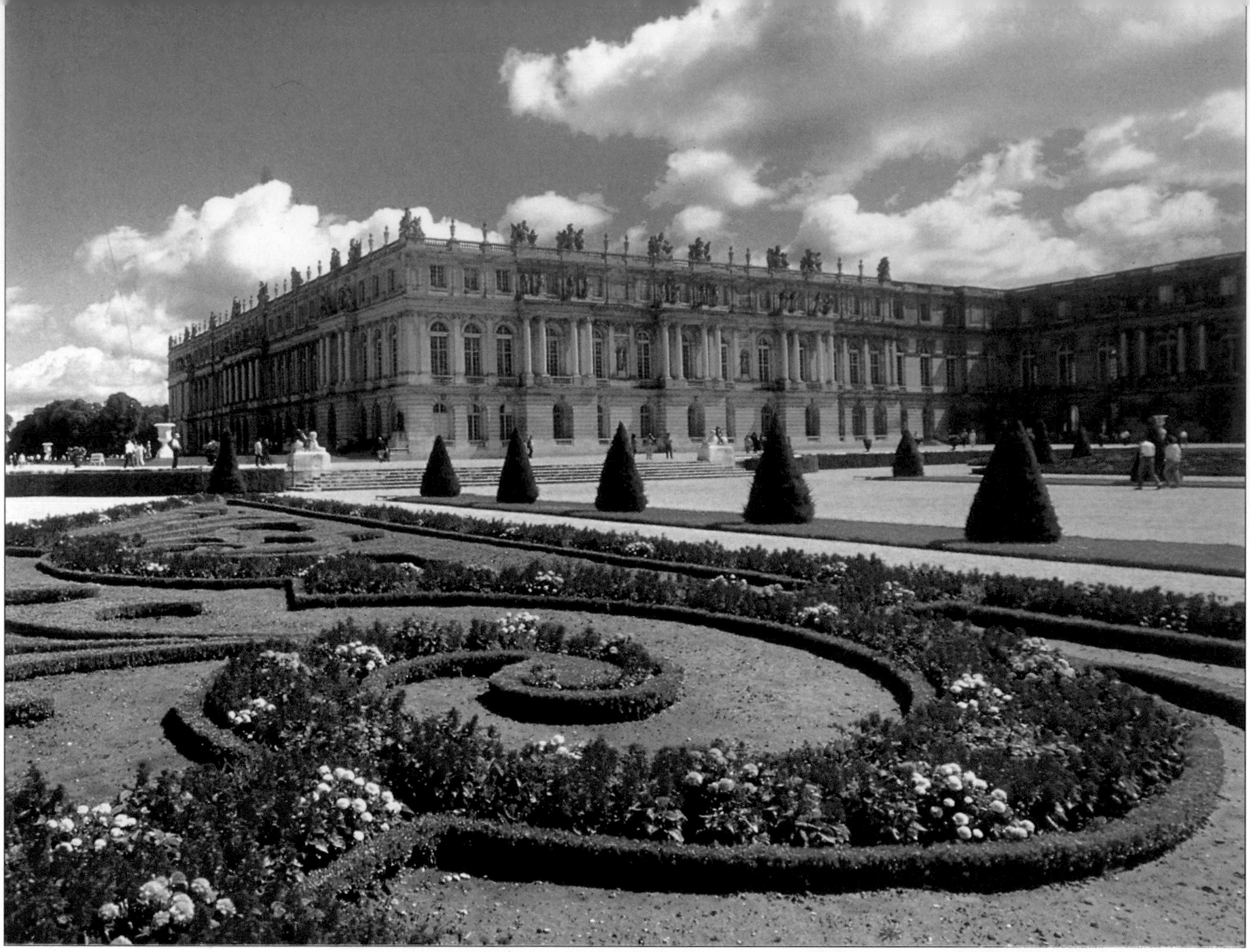

Tony Craddock/Tony Stone Worldwide

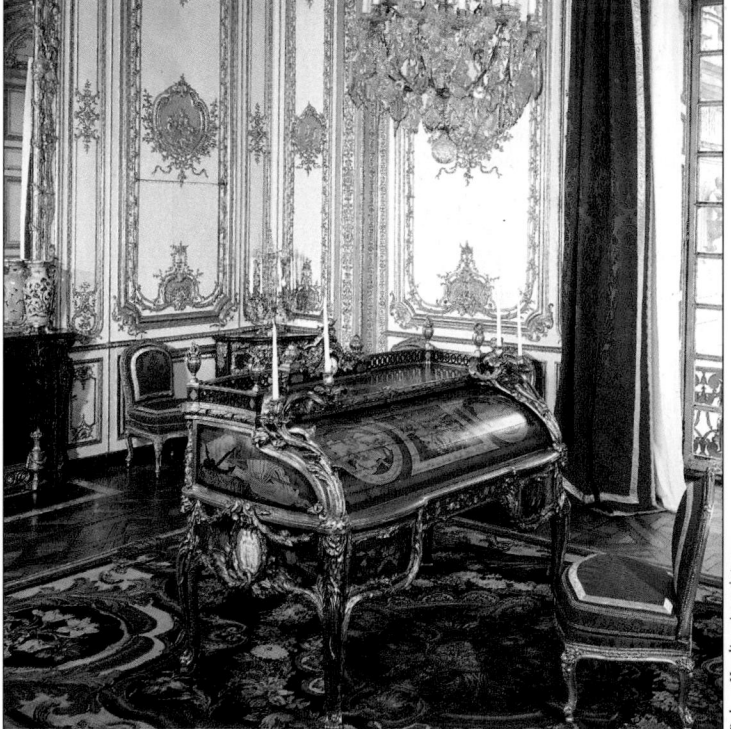

♔ Versailles was characterised by formal gardens and airy open spaces, but in the days of Louis XV, these were often filled with the public, who were allowed almost unrestricted access. Originally laid out by André Le Nôtre, the gardens set a fashion which was imitated by noble houses throughout Europe

© R.M.N.

♔ The King's ***cabinet de travail***, or study, in the palace of Versailles. The centrepiece of the room is his personal desk, the ***Bureau du Roi***, ordered in 1760 and decorated with marquetry and ormolu in the style known as Louis Quinze. The room also displays a fine Savonnerie carpet and the walls are decorated with gilt ***boiseries*** by Verberckt

Robert Harding Associates

♔ The ***Cabinet de la Pendule*** in the ***Petits Appartements*** of the King ***right*** was named after the clock, which was made by Passemant in 1749. These light, airy apartment rooms on the second floor were far smaller and more intimate than the official staterooms. They offered Louis a welcome retreat from the press of courtiers and connected directly to the apartment of his mistress

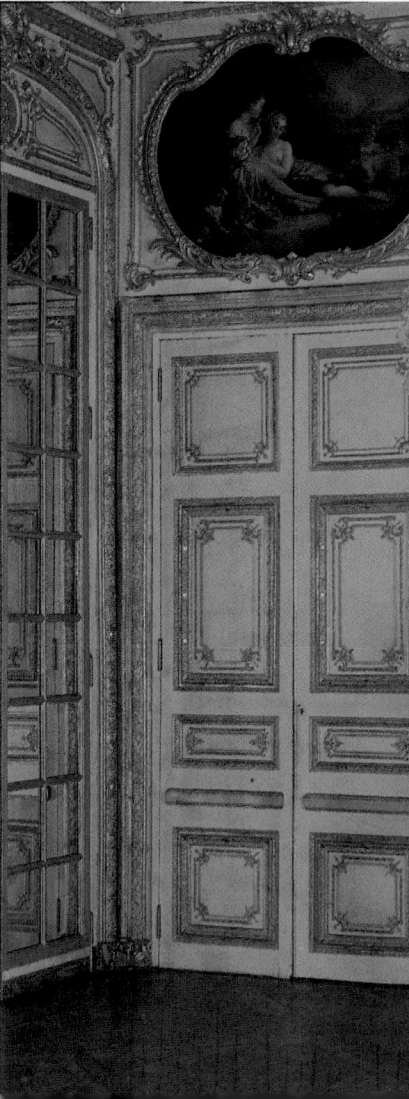

♛ Water from one of Versailles' many fountains was a constant accompaniment throughout the gardens. 30,000 workmen were employed to level and drain the grounds – and to supply the enormous quantities of water required, a pump was constructed to raise water from the Seine into a specially built acqueduct

♛ Set in splendid rural isolation, Fontainebleau *above* was the focus of the annual retreat, called the *voyage*. The château was always important in the life of the court – Louis and Maria Leczinska were married there in 1725. It was substantially extended in 1738 with a new wing built by Jacques Ange Gabriel and known as the *Louis Quinze*. Madame de Pompadour had her own apartments there

♛ Part of the modernisation programme at Fontainebleau, the imposing *Salle de Conseil*, or King's Council Chamber *above*, was decorated by Boucher and Carle Van Loo in the rococo style. The room was extended in 1773, near the end of Louis XV's reign, by the addition of a new bay

♛ The *Galerie de François I* at Fontainebleau *left* shows the more sober style of the old palace. 64 metres long, it was built between 1528-44 and decorated by Il Rosso, an Italian who with his countryman Francesco Pomadiccio laid the foundations of the French artistic tradition. Very little else remained from this period of the palace

UNBROKEN AFFECTION

DESPITE A RADICAL CHANGE IN THEIR RELATIONSHIP, MADAME DE POMPADOUR REMAINED AT THE CENTRE OF THE KING'S LIFE. THEIR LOVE SURVIVED COURT INTRIGUES AND LOUIS' CASUAL AMOURS – BUT NOT WITHOUT SOME ANXIOUS MOMENTS

C. van Loo: Louis XV. Versailles/Lauros-Giraudon

👑 *King Louis XV*, above, *still an ardent lover, painted by Carle van Loo*

👑 *By 1758, when the portrait*, right, *was painted, the physical relationship was over*

At some time in the early 1750s, Louis XV and Madame de Pompadour ceased to be lovers. This side of their relationship had always caused difficulties, as Louis was an exceptionally ardent lover whereas the Marquise admitted to being physically cold. She regretted the fact, for 'I adore that man, and I long to please him, but he thinks I'm fearfully cold.' At times her desperation to please had led her to try quack medicines, in an effort to 'warm herself up'. Not surprisingly, they had no effect and she had to be weaned off these concoctions for the sake of her health.

With the years, the problems grew worse, for she had never been robust. A strenuous life and a series of miscarriages made her health still more uncertain. Louis was now in his forties – in 18th-century terms the threshold of old age – and had begun to feel restless. Whether there was a genuine crisis between them or just a civilized agreement, the great change was made. The 'affair' was over and Louis was free to take his pleasures elsewhere.

A new relationship

For almost any other royal mistress, this would have meant an end to the relationship and expulsion from the court. But Louis continued to love her, and – perhaps more important – still found her company delightful and her apartments the most pleasant of all. The apartments themselves were changed: early in 1752 the Marquise moved closer to Louis on the ground floor. Her new quarters were much grander, giving notice that she was as high as ever in the royal favour. And, just to make the matter clear beyond doubt, the King granted her the title of Duchess.

With characteristic restraint, she assumed the heraldry of her new rank but continued to use the title Marquise. This, she felt was preferable to setting herself against the haughty dukes and duchesses of ancient pedigree.

PLEASURES OF THE DEER PARK

Even in Louis XV's lifetime, dark rumours circulated about his sex life. It was said that his agents kidnapped girls from the streets of Paris and installed them in the house in the Deer Park – the villa in Versailles. The villa, they said, was the King's personal harem, where he indulged in frightful orgies with his friends. The facts, rather less exciting, are that Louis took his pleasures quietly enough in the palace or at the villa, named after the deer park that had once occupied the land.

The girls themselves were told that their patron was a Polish nobleman related to the Queen, and when Louis tired of any of them they were sent away with generous dowries. The only one of these girls to capture the King's imagination was Louise O'Murphy, whose endearing charms are quite obvious in the famous paintings by Boucher. One diarist noted that, 'The King is more and more in love with the little Morfi. She amuses him and that's important.' Louise had at least two children by the King and began to seem like a fixture until she became overconfident and insolently touched on his relationship with Madame de Pompadour. When she asked, 'How are things between you and the old lady?' Louis coldly dismissed her from his life immediately.

Meanwhile, Louis had found a practical, if somewhat unpalatable, way of satisfying his physical needs. His valet de chambre, Lebel, procured healthy and attractive young working girls from Paris and installed them in a villa, known as the Deer Park, in the town of Versailles, where the King visited them as and when he pleased. The girls satisfied the King's senses but made no demands on his emotions. The situation suited Madame de Pompadour; 'It's his heart I want,' she told Madame de Hausset, 'and those ignorant little girls won't steal it from me.'

It was even rumoured that she vetted new arrivals; it was certainly true that she made the arrangements when a girl bore the King's baby. Louise O'Murphy, daughter of an Irish cobbler,

'I adore that man, and I long to please him, but he thinks I'm fearfully cold'

MADAME DE POMPADOUR

was the only one who kept the King's interest for long. Her doll-like features and enticing body appear in many pictures by the court painter, Boucher, who was the first to 'discover' her – but one rude remark about Madame de Pompadour was enough to make Louis send her packing.

The regal lady

In her new apartments, the reigning mistress seemed more like a queen than a duchess. When speaking, she openly used 'we' – coupling herself with the King. Since her bedroom was not furnished with chairs – deliberately, of course – even the most distinguished visitors were obliged to stand, as if in the presence of a royal personage. And her retinue of servants became so large that there was not enough room for them at the palace, and they had to be accommodated in a special mansion in the town of Versailles.

Because of her unrestricted access to the King's heart, mind and purse, Madame de Pompadour was besieged by people seeking privileges, places and pensions – which at Versailles meant almost everybody. Family and friends came first, and contemporaries would have been astonished had it been otherwise. The fatherly de Tournehem was director of the King's buildings, and when he died in December 1751 he was succeeded by the Marquise's brother Abel, soon to be Marquis de Marigny. More conscientious than many others in her position, Madame de Pompadour had made sure that her brother received thorough training before he began.

Tocque: Marquis de Marigny. Versailles/ Lauros-Giraudon

♛ *Louise O'Murphy, called* Morfi *by the French, painted by François Boucher. As mistress to Louis XV, she bore him several children but was eventually to lose his favour because of a rude remark about Madame de Pompadour*

♛ *Madame de Pompadour's brother, Abel François Poisson de Vandières, Marquis de Marigny (1727-1781). Thanks to his sister's position, he succeeded Le Normant de Tournehem as director of the King's buildings*

ADVENTURERS AT COURT

The 18th century was the age of gifted, shady adventurers, and the court of Versailles proved curiously susceptible to their wiles. The self-styled Comte de St Germain claimed to be at least 2,000 years old and would refer casually to his encounters with Alexander the Great and Jesus. He cast Madame de Pompadour's horoscope and astonished Louis by appearing to fuse three small diamonds into a single large one. The King gave him a pension, an alchemist's laboratory, and even employed him as a diplomatic agent. He was shrewd enough to move on to a new court before he was found out, and lived until 1784.

An equally engaging and much-travelled rascal, Giovanni Casanova, is now remembered for the memoirs in which he recounts his wanderings, occult impostures, imprisonments and *amours*. For a time, he was director of the French state lottery and, although he never became part of the court, he left a vivid outsider's view of the royal family's public life and was present at the execution of Louis' would-be assassin.

Mansell Collection

♔ Madame de Pompadour with her daughter, Alexandrine d'Etioles, known affectionately as Fan-fan. Alexandrine was to die at the age of ten of convulsions – almost certainly caused by appendicitis – at the convent where she was being educated. She died before her mother could reach her. Her death was a crushing blow for old Poisson, who died four days later, and for Madame de Pompadour, who never really recovered from it

However regal the airs she now gave herself, the Marquise remained kindly and obliging. Among many she helped were her friend Voltaire, and writers who at that time often fell foul of the church and censorship. But, like all patrons, she found that there were never enough good things to go round, and that refusal, however gracious, added another name to her long list of enemies.

While the King stood by her, she was invulnerable but she could never be completely sure of him. The 'ignorant little girls' in the Deer Park were not a serious threat, but a lady of the court who played her cards cleverly might influence him so thoroughly that he would promise her anything. This eventuality occurred as early as 1752, when the pretty 18-year-old Madame de Choiseul led Louis a maddening dance, surrendering only when he declared that he was willing to send Madame de Pompadour away.

He might have felt obliged to keep his word had Madame de Choiseul not made a fatal mistake. One day she showed a letter she had received from the King to her cousin, the Comte

de Stainville. Madame de Choiseul had never dreamed that he was anything but an ally, but de Stainville showed it to Madame de Pompadour, whom he knew to be distraught about the affair. The letter revealed that Madame de Choiseul was pregnant, and Madame de Pompadour, fearful of losing both the King's devotion and her own position, flew into a rage and confronted him. Louis was remorseful and furious with his new mistress, who promptly had to leave the court.

Devotion and danger
The King proved his love for the Marquise when her daughter died in 1754, spending hours by her bedside in an attempt to console her – an extraordinary act of devotion on the part of a man who was so painfully embarrassed by other people's grief. Yet despite his deep affection, he still gave the Marquise cause to doubt his feelings.

Barely a year after the death of her daughter, the King became involved with the Marquise de Coislin. It did not last but, for a time, Madame de Pompadour suffered acutely from uncertainty

Bonham's, London/Bridgeman

THE BEAUTY OF SÈVRES

One of Louis XV and Madame de Pompadour's most enduring legacies was the Sèvres porcelain factory, celebrated for the brilliant royal blues and gilding of its wares. Long the secret of the East, the formula for making fine porcelain was discovered at Meissen in Saxony at the beginning of the 18th century – an age which, above all others, took pleasure in delicacy, lightness and novelty.

A porcelain works was established at Vincennes in 1738, but it was struggling until 1751, when the King made a substantial investment in it. Two years later it moved to Sèvres, close to Madame de Pompadour's favourite Château de Bellevue.

Vincennes-Sèvres was famous for its lifelike porcelain flowers, and on one occasion the King visited Bellevue in mid-winter to find an entire garden of spring and summer flowers – all, on closer inspection, products of Sèvres.

As the arbiter of French fashion, the Marquise made Sèvres porcelain indispensable in every aristocratic household – and later when the factory became an entirely royal concern, she and the King had a financial as well as an artistic incentive for promoting Sèvres as forcefully as possible.

The factory – which is still in operation – never looked back and, appropriately enough, one of its most popular background colours – a beautiful deep pink – is known today as *rose Pompadour.*

Giraudon

⚜ *Madame de Choiseul, the pretty, but foolish 18-year-old whom Madame de Pompadour introduced to the King. She was perhaps not wise to have thrown them together; a great deal of flirtation ensued, which ended in disgrace for the new mistress*

about Louis' intentions. 'You don't know the King,' she confided to her maid. 'If he was going to put her in my room this very night, he'd still be cold to her and friendly to me in public.' Such remarks lift the curtain a little on the state of tension in which she must always have lived.

As well as coping with enemies at court, Madame de Pompadour had come to terms with the fact that the French people hated her. This was not unexpected, since royal mistresses were always unpopular. Rather than hold the King himself responsible for anything that went wrong, people blamed the bad counsellors and ambitious women around him, consoling themselves with the thought that His Majesty would find out what was going on and put matters right.

So when the royal mistress ventured out, mud was thrown at 'La Pompadour's' coach, just as it had been thrown at those of Madame de Châteauroux and other predecessors. In 1749, an official trip to Le Hâvre caused such an outcry that the Marquise contented herself from then on with the familiar round of visits to royal houses

and her own residences. And after unpleasant incidents in the capital, she never again went to Paris unless it was absolutely unavoidable.

A gathering storm

More serious were signs that even the King was no longer beyond criticism. Much of Louis' reign was taken up with endless, complicated struggles between the Crown, the Church and Parliament, who were all jealously bent on maintaining their privileges.

Meanwhile, neither war nor peace seemed to benefit the populace, which was often close to famine, and resentment began to focus on the inhabitants of Versailles and their outrageous extravagances – a wave of feeling that was to culminate in the French Revolution of 1789. Stories circulated in the capital, exaggerated at every telling, that pictured the King as a monster of depravity. As a new and unpopular war against England broke out, discontent grew even more marked, and one man took it upon himself to do something about it – with a small knife.

ROCOCO ART

It was said that few people since the world began have owned so many beautiful things as Madame de Pompadour. Under her patronage, French art and craftsmanship flourished as never before, and it was a tragedy for the national heritage when her personal collection was dispersed after her death. Few of the pieces which she owned remain, but the contemporary examples shown here are typical of the Rococo style that she and Louis did so much to foster

A Louis XV silver tureen by Juste Aurièle Meissonier *below*. Although not one of Madame de Pompadour's own pieces, the fish motif – a play on her maiden name 'Poisson' – was one of her favourites. Whenever a fine example came the King's way, he would have it presented to her, and she even signed her own engravings with a stylised fish

The very influential Louis XV commode *below* was made by Bernard van Riesenburgh and carries an ormolu mantel clock stamped St Germain and Le Roy of Paris. One of a pair, the commode is veneered with marquetry patterns in tulipwood and kingwood, mounted with scrolling ormolu foliage. The bowed 'bombe' front is characteristic of the period

Private Collection/Bridgeman

Christie's, London/Bridgeman

♛ An enamelled box *below* set with pearls and small jewels. Made in the mid-18th Century, this displays the delicacy and detail which typify contemporary French taste

♛ A gold snuff box *left* with miniatures of the château at Bellevue by Louis-Nicolas van Blarenberghe. Bellevue was owned and extensively rebuilt by Madame de Pompadour, but sold to the King in 1757

♛ This pot-pourri vase and cover *above* are in Chinese 'mirror black' porcelain with ormolu mounts. Ormolu, a gilt metal alloy, was one of the characteristic materials of the period, while Chinese decorative work, called *chinoiserie*, was among the important influences on contemporary style

♛ Fans *left* were an essential accessory for high-born ladies and were frequently very ornate. This fine example from 1769 depicts an illegitimate child of Louis XV being presented to his father at court

FAITHFUL TO THE END

TO THE END OF HER LIFE THE MARQUISE ACTED AS THE KING'S LOYAL HELPMEET. LONELY AFTER HER DEATH, LOUIS BEGAN A LIAISON WITH THE LOVELY MADAME DU BARRY. BUT NOTHING COULD REPLACE HIS 'SINCERE AND TENDER POMPADOUR'

Early in the evening of 5 January 1757, Louis XV was leaving Versailles when a man emerged from the crowd, struck him, and walked away. When he had recovered from his surprise, the King realized that he was covered with blood and quickly had himself taken back into the palace. Over the next few hours he was given absolution, confessed, and publicly apologized to his wife and children for his past conduct.

It was all curiously similar to the events at Metz a dozen years earlier, although this time Louis' sins were not broadcast in every French parish church. As at Metz, the danger proved to be exaggerated. Delivered with the smaller blade of a penknife through layers of winter clothing, the wound was shallow. Fortunately the knife had not poisoned. When arrested, the would-be assassin, a fellow named Damiens, declared he simply wanted to 'bring the King to his senses'.

Louis made a rapid physical recovery, but remained strangely pensive for days; as at Metz, the Queen, his children, and those who hated Madame de Pompadour all hoped that he would have a permanent change of heart.

The Marquise could not go to Louis, even after he had recovered, without being summoned; and no summons came. Seeing him surrounded by her enemies, she despaired; and when a false friend told her he was sure that the King wished her to leave Versailles for good, she almost committed the fatal mistake of complying. 'He who leaves the table, loses the game', said a true friend, who persuaded her to wait.

♛ *Damiens, in the act of attacking the King. Louis was not badly hurt and made a good recovery, but he had received a severe mental shock. As a result, he became convinced that Damiens was acting for the entire French nation, who now hated him*

Mansell Collection

Eventually, Louis slipped away to see her and unburdened himself of the feelings that were weighing him down. He was convinced that Damiens had acted on behalf of the French people, who had come to hate him. Magically, Madame de Pompadour succeeded in convincing him that Damiens was a solitary madman and that he, the King, was still Louis the Well-Beloved. This was not entirely true, but the assassination attempt had caused a revulsion of feeling in favour of the King throughout the country; so Madame de Pompadour's words did have an air of truth about them. And for the King, having seen his mistress again, he felt he was cured; so life at Versailles could resume its normal pattern.

A settled existence

Nothing, it seemed, could dull the King's affection for the Marquise; evidently she still had an extraordinary power over Louis, even though her youthful looks had faded. Having ceased to sin with the King, she proceeded to cancel the other score against he, her desertion of Le Normant d'Etioles, by offering to return to him. What she was hoping for was a polite refusal, which was duly received. Now, as a virtuous,

'He who leaves the table, loses the game'

A FRIEND TO MADAME DE POMPADOUR

rejected wife, she was considered acceptable in the eyes of the church and eligible to become one of the social and moral elite as Lady in waiting to the Queen. As portraits from this period show, she began to dress in a slightly matronly fashion, wearing a cap; but occasional rumours that she had given up using cosmetics always proved to be unfounded!

The power behind the throne

She had also begun to take a hand in politics. Encouraged by Louis' odd taste for conducting negotiations behind his ministers' backs, she played a large part in arranging an alliance with France's old enemy, Austria, that changed the diplomatic map of Europe. Her old friend the Abbé de Bernis was also involved, and emerged, effectively, as Foreign Minister of France. The

Drouais: Mme de Pompadour, Musée Condé, Chantilly/Giraudon/Bridgeman

♛ *Madame de Pompadour was 42 when she died, and remained actively involved in all the King's affairs until her final illness. This, one of her last portraits, was painted by François-Hubert Drouais, and probably completed after her death*

👑 *On 20 June 1763, the King attended the inauguration of the Place Louis XV in Paris, designed by Jacques Gabriel. It was dominated by a splendid equestrian statue of the King with an allegorical figure at each corner, representing Force, Prudence, Justice and Peace. The statue was destroyed at the Revolution and the square is now called the Place de la Concorde. A small bronze copy of the statue can be seen at Versailles. Madame de Pompadour made one of her last public appearances at this event; it was not well received by the crowd*

Jean-Loup Charmet

Fotomas Index

👑 *The Marquise played a large part in arranging the alliance between France and Austria – an unfortunate consequence of which was the Seven Years War. This is an allegorical engraving done by Madame de Pompadour herself, depicting the treaty agreement*

alliance proved to be the prelude to a great war in which France fought Britain overseas and Prussia on the Continent.

This, the Seven Years War (1756-63), was the most serious conflict of Louis' reign and he became more preoccupied with decision-making than ever before. As usual. Madame de Pompadour adapted to the situation, turning her apartments into a map- and paper-strewn war office, and acting as the King's secretary – some even said Prime Minister. The only remnant of her old gaiety was her habit of marking the positions of armies on the maps with beauty spots rather than flagged pins!

Unfortunately, the war turned into a series of disasters for the French army. Futile, sometimes humiliating campaigns were undertaken in Europe, while the provinces in Canada and India were lost for good to the British. The Abbé de Bernis was soon replaced by a much more able minister, the Duc de Choiseul (none other than the Comte de Stainville who had served Madame de Pompadour so well a few years earlier). De Choiseul took over many of the burdens which had been the Marquise's, but the peace, when it came at last, was far from glorious.

The final years

All this saddened the final years of Madame de Pompadour's 'reign' at Versailles, which she knew to be coming to its close. She was frequently confined to bed now with throat and chest ailments, probably symptomatic of tuberculosis or lung cancer. Although she made preparations to retire from the court, Louis would not hear of it. But before the question seemed worth discussing seriously, it was too late. Madame de Pompadour was dying.

The Marquise made a final public appearance – which was not well received by Parisians – at the opening of the Place Louis XV, better known since the French Revolution as the Place de la Concorde. Shortly afterwards, she was taken ill at Choisy and, lungs awash with liquid and coughing incessantly, began the final struggle. Louis, violating the normally accepted rule that only royalty might die at Versailles, had brought her to the palace.

Even Madame de Pompadour's enemies admired the fortitude with which she bore herself at the end. Seated upright in a chair (she could no longer breathe lying down), with a touch of rouge to give her colour, she called all

J.M. van Loo: Louis XV, Musee de Beaux Arts, Rennes/Giraudon

'The end is coming now. Leave me to my soul, my women and my priest'

MADAME DE POMPADOUR

her friends to her and said gracious farewells to each of them. Louis was there constantly, almost to the last – for once she had confessed to the priest, she could no longer see the man who had been her lover and friend for twenty years.

Her final word on the relationship was spoken to the Duc de Choiseul, by now one of her dearest friends. She confided to him that she had always loved the King but had never really understood him as his character was 'indecipherable'. The next day, 15 April 1764, she told Choiseul and others who remained, 'The end is coming now. Leave me to my soul, my women and the priest.'

When the priest nevertheless seemed to be going, she said to him, 'One moment, Monsieur le Curé: we'll leave together.' And she died. She was 42 years old.

Protocol observed

There was no relaxation of the rule that corpses could not remain in the palace. Madame de Pompadour's body was placed on a stretcher, covered with a sheet, and hurried to her house in the town of Versailles. In her will she had directed that she was to be buried with her little daughter in a convent on the Place Vendôme in Paris. Two days after her death, the *cortège* left Versailles in a howling storm. The King could not accompany it: it was yet another of those things that were simply not done. 'The Marquise has bad weather for her journey,' he remarked.

Although the shutters had been closed so as to spare him the sight, Louis went out on to the balcony and watched in silence as the funeral procession passed down the Avenue de Paris. When it was finally lost to sight, he re-entered his room. Two large teardrops flowed slowly down his cheeks. Then he said, 'These are the only tributes I can pay her.'

♛ A portrait of the ageing Louis XV by Louis Michel van Loo. Van Loo (normally called Michel) lived from 1707 to 1771 and like his brother Carle was a leading artist of the period who profited by the patronage which still flourished in the later years of Madame de Pompadour and King Louis XV

MADAME DU BARRY

Louis XV's young and beautiful mistress can truly be said to have risen from obscurity; even her date of birth is not certain. Her origins were hardly distinguished.

Christened Jeanne, she was the illegitimate daughter of Anne Bécu, born at Vaucouleurs and brought to Paris, where her mother married. Jeanne was educated at a convent. In her teens she worked at a hairdresser's and drifted from lover to lover until she met the Chevalier du Barry, who made her the star attraction of a gambling den catering to the upper classes.

When she caught the King's eye, the Chevalier (who was already married) arranged instant rank and respectability for her with a wedding to his brother, the Comte du Barry, and financed her appearance in good society and presentation at court. The gamble paid handsome dividends, for during her reign as Louis' mistress, Madame du Barry accumulated a fortune.

The King's death immediately ended this career, and Madame du Barry left Versailles as soon as he had said his farewells to her. Unluckily for her, she lived to see the French Revolution and, as a hated aristo was dragged out of retirement and guillotined in 1793.

Drouais: Mme du Barry, Prado, Madrid/Bridgeman

LOUIS XVI AND MARIE ANTOINETTE

Louis XV's son died the year after Madame de Pompadour, and his 11-year-old grandson became the new Dauphin. In 1770, a clumsy, well-meaning young man, he married the Austrian princess Marie Antoinette, and in 1774 succeeded his grandfather as King Louis XVI. Happier with his hobbies than politics, he failed to solve France's chronic problems. Virtual bankruptcy in 1789 set in motion the French Revolution, the fall of the monarchy and the execution of Louis himself in 1793.

His queen, Marie Antoinette, was pretty, extravagant and frivolous. Ignoring public duties, she enjoyed play-acting the squire's wife at the *Petit Hameau*, a mock-village in the grounds of Versailles. Although sexual difficulties on Louis' part prevented consummation of their marriage for years, they eventually had children and lived amicably. However, her reputation was damaged by scandal and she became very unpopular. She may not have said 'Let them eat cake' when the people had no bread, but it was significant that it was believed. She followed Louis to the scaffold in 1793.

Louis XV had ten more years to live. It was obvious that he missed the Marquise, and none of her proposed successors lasted very long. Four years passed, during which the Dauphin and the Queen died – events that perhaps encouraged the ageing King to throw off all restraint. His latest mistress was young and lovely but had a lurid past that would once have made her presentation at court unthinkable. Now Madame du Barry, born of an unknown father, became the new *Maitresse en Titre*, spending money at a rate that made Madame de Pompadour' purchases seem positively thrifty.

The King was not in love with her, but told his close friends that he had never experienced such skillful love-making, and that Madame du Barry was the only woman who could make him forget that he was 60. When the Duc de Choiseul complained of her, Louis told him with brutal frankness, 'She is pretty, she satisfies me, that is enough.' Less capable than ever of distinguishing between his personal interests

and the needs of the state, the King resolved the conflict by dismissing the able de Choiseul.

None of France's problems were solved during Louis' last years. The King himself was happiest when he could withdraw from the court, accompanied by Madame du Barry, to the Petit Trianon, an elegant little house in the park at Versailles; ironically, it had been commissioned by the King and Madame de Pompadour, who died before it was finished. It was here, while down with a fever, that the first tell-tale blotches appeared on his face. They were symptoms of smallpox – a scourge that ruined the looks of pretty women and carried off the very young and the old. Louis was 64.

Once more, protocol triumphed: it would not do for a King of France to die anywhere but Versailles. Reluctantly Louis allowed himself to be carried to a coach and driven across the park to the palace. There he lingered, long enough to infect 50 people.

Then, like Madame de Pompadour before him, he sent his lover away and made his peace with God. On 10 May 1774, Louis XV died. The corridors of Versailles resounded with a noise like thunder as courtiers rushed to hail Louis XVI and Marie Antoinette, the two doomed young sovereigns of France.

♚ *The* Fleur de France *by Glokeur de Surchamps. Set in a fleur-de-lis frame, it forms a genealogical tree with 13 miniatures showing Louis XV and his descendants*